Linda Grant was born in Liverpool and now lives in London. Her first novel, *The Cast Iron Shore*, won the David Higham First Novel Prize and was shortlisted for the Guardian Fiction Prize. Her second novel, *When I Lived in Modern Times*, won the Orange Prize for Fiction. *Still Here* was longlisted for the Man Booker Prize. She is also the author of *Sexing the Millennium: A Political History of the Sexual Revolution* and *Remind Me Who I Am, Again*, a family memoir.

THE PEOPLE ON THE STREET

A WRITER'S VIEW OF ISRAEL

LINDA GRANT

Virago

VIRAGO

First published in Great Britain in March 2006 by Virago Press
Reprinted 2006

A CIP catalogue record for this book
is available from the British Library.

ISBN 1 84408 254 7

Typeset in Goudy by M Rules
Printed and bound in Great Britain by
Clays Ltd, St Ives plc

Virago Press
An imprint of
Time Warner Book Group UK
Brettenham House
Lancaster Place
London WC2E 7EN

www.virago.co.uk

For Judah Passow

Here is a square where everybody meets.
Here is a doorway through which troops have pressed.
Here is a yard with women hanging sheets.

George Szirtes, from *Reel*.

Ben Yehuda

One day I was walking along the street in Tel Aviv, when I got a call on my cellphone: 'Check out the news, they're saying Saddam has been captured.'

'Hey,' I said, walking into my café, because everyone in the country has 'their' café, where they drink coffee, read the papers, eat cake, argue about football and politics and take offence and storm out in a huff, then come back the next day for more of the same, for years on end; the same table, the same slice of chocolate torte, the same faces, everyone ready for a row.

'I just heard Saddam has been captured,' I said, sitting down.

'What?'

The waiter was out like a shot and the men abandoned their espressos and milky lattes and poppy seed cookies and they all followed him onto the street and into the convenience store where a crowd was watching CNN.

Everyone gasped. A dishevelled dirty grey-bearded old man was being pulled out of a hole in the ground. Where was the glossy black hair, the important moustache, the adoring crowds? '*Oy, be'emet*,' someone said, and everyone turned round and glared at her. Expressions of pity were out of place today, this was the monster who had sent his scud missiles raining down on the Tel Aviv suburb of Ramat Gan during the first Gulf War and all they had for protection were the Americans, who had set up their Patriot missile battery on top of the Iria rubbish tip and landfill site which disfigures the horizon on the highway between the city and the airport.

'*In arabkum ars!*' a man shouted, raising his fist at the screen and had Saddam been able to hear through the glass, he would have known exactly what was being said, because it was Arabic. '*Your father is a pimp.*'

I watched tv for a while with them, then they switched from CNN to a Hebrew channel and I decided to go home.

I walked past the falafel café where the man with tight black curls fried balls of chickpeas all day long and pushed them into pita breads, with a selection of pickles and tahina. He had a huge smile on his face. I had never before seen him so pleased. It was hard, oily work in there, frying all day long.

'You look happy.'

'I am. You heard that Saddam's been captured?'

'I know, I just saw it on tv up the street.'

'It's true that he was in a hole in the ground with a big beard?'

'Yes.'

'Oh my god, I can't wait to get home and see that. I don't have a tv here, just a radio and I haven't got anyone to mind the store while I run out to have a look.' He looked up at the clock on the wall. 'Six more hours!'

'Let me take a guess,' I said, 'Are you from Iraq?'

The street was full of Iraqis: I had already had a long conversation with the silversmith from the mountains of the Kurdish north who, at the weekends, went hiking in the West Bank out of longing for the landscape of his lost childhood, still tasting in his mouth the meals his mother made which, he told me, was the same food the Babylonian exiles ate in the Bible.

'Yes,' said the falafel man, 'I'm from Baghdad, I was born there.'

'When did you come to Israel?'

'When I was seven years old, with my parents in 1950, but my father never liked it here and in 1959 we left. Guess where he took us?'

'America?'

'No.'

'France?'

'No.'

'Berlin?'

'Teheran.' He slapped the side of his head with his hand. 'Jews! *Jews!*'

Jews. Indeed.

In October 2003 I came to Tel Aviv and stayed four months in an apartment round the corner from the falafel stand and café and convenience store. It was in a long, low, four-storey building, which extended along the street with two front doors leading to two separate sets of stairs united by a common hallway, surrounded by a dry shady cactus garden, with palms and sand and cats and hot smells of decaying leaves and overflowing garbage cans. Across the street hibiscus bushes overflowed with red trumpet flowers. I was in the dead centre of what they still sometimes call the White City, and the building had some of the features of the Bauhaus style – of a city that had been founded in 1909, but mostly constructed in a hurry between 1933 and 1939. Mass immigration from Europe created a panicky need for new homes, designed by refugee architects trained in the newest techniques of building with minimum decoration in the cheapest material available: concrete.

They had created a whole Bauhaus town on the shores of the Mediterranean Middle East, white boxes with curved balconies resembling the prows of ships, thrusting out along the street as if they longed for the sea, apartments where refugees bent their heads over books and listened to records on their gramophones, absorbed in Schiller and Schoenberg, still not quite comprehending that central European civilisation was up to its neck in blood; while in the apartment below, a gangster from Odessa was planning the heist of a jewellery store on the Allenby Road, and his girlfriend bent over a sink, dyeing her hair.

I came to Tel Aviv from London to write a novel and still it isn't written. In my novel there was a country to which immigrants arrived from all over the world. You could have placed it in the middle of the Antarctic Ocean with only polar bears and penguins for enemies and still it would have been a very difficult place with a lot of unique problems. It was a country made up of those who had been scared and hurt and threatened, a land of exiles from suffering, and I did not think it would be very pleasant, full of nice, warm, accommodating people. In my novel, I was also trying to find out how various forms of pleasure can be applied to pain, to make it better.

The country was not Israel, and the city was not Tel Aviv, but somewhere that existed in my imagination, my own homeland, my own hometown that was not on any map, except the intimate geography of my self.

I was devastated when no one believed me. It *was* Israel, it *was* Tel Aviv, they insisted, it had to be, despite the invented topography and history. I don't know what got inside me that I wanted to write this book. I suppose I was trying to work out something about Jews, because if I could get that figured out, I might understand something about myself, about why I behave this way and not that . . . and to be honest, because I like stories and the Jewish story seemed to me, and still does, the story to beat them all. Well, perhaps not the Odyssey and Iliad, but it is a long tale that winds through many countries, and contains so many tricky problems and baffling concepts: such as what a Jew is in the first place, since you can have a Jew like me, with no religion at all, and a Jew from Ethiopia who is black, and a Jew from Romania who is blond and a Jew who is a convert from Christianity – so that I sometimes think that the root cause of anti-Semitism is that Jews drive other people mad because they can't work out who or what we are, and what category to place us in, so we are both the subject and originator of endless rows.

There are two places in the world that are full of Jews: New York and Israel. I am not an American; life for me would probably have been easier had I been born in an apartment building on the Upper West Side, of Democrat-voting parents who worshipped Roosevelt, and had lifetime membership cards to the New York Public Library, but that's not my story. My family have been trying to make it over the Atlantic since 1904, never quite getting there, or for some reason, coming back again, and, at this moment, a branch of it is dithering about Green Cards, but I'm still stuck on the other side, a category error, a British Jew, when everyone knows that the British are tactful, decorous, well-mannered, prudent, prone to meaningful silences, and Jews are – well, the opposite.

So I found myself, in my forties, drawn to Israel, not out of Zionism or interest in the Middle East conflict, but because the moment I put my foot down there, everything was half familiar. I had half the story already inside my head, and was avid and eager to learn the rest.

I came to write a novel, not to be a reporter or an activist. I sat in my apartment and tapped away on my laptop. In the afternoons and evenings I walked, saw friends, ventured forth. I did some journalism, and after I left I returned twice, once to write about the settlers of Gaza who were about to be 'disengaged' from their houses, and another visit, with someone who told me a different story, but we'll come to that later. Mainly what I did was look, and ask some questions, and listen, and in an abdication or indeed abnegation of Jewishness, tried not to venture an opinion, because in this part of the world opinions have become so debased a currency on the market place, there's such a glut of them, the inflation rate is so high, that they'll hardly buy you a Jaffa orange.

The apartment was small, just a room with a long kitchen leading off it, a bathroom, and an alcove taken up mainly by the bed. It was really noisy outside, the air was always cracking. From five in the morning the motorised grinders of the garbage trucks thudded and roared through the streets, and after that the slamming doors, cars starting up, sirens of police cars, arguments between neighbours, the loud humming of the air conditioning units, the rag and bone man on his horse and cart with the flag waving above the horse's arse on high days and holidays, crying out for iron in the echoing streets.* And always that great atonal symphony of the cellphone because this is the country which has the highest per capita use in the world.

The windows at one side overlooked someone's balcony, with a woman who sat out in the mornings drying her hair; on the other side I could see, hear and smell the clanking steamy kitchens

*'The rag and bone men in Israel call out, *Alte Zakhen* ("old things" in Yiddish), so that's what they are called. Most of the *alte zakhen* men these days are Arabs, still screaming out the same two Yiddish words, with an Arab accent.' (Ophir Wright, email to LG)

of the Grand Hotel Deborah; and on the third, I overlooked Gordon Street, with an aesthetician's studio specialising in manicures, pedicures and facials carried out by a hefty, raddled Russian woman; a currency exchange store; a jeweller, a thin brown woman with glasses; and a taxi company whose dispatcher was one of those types manufactured in a plant somewhere in the Ukraine which produces a universal unit: the women with the hard menopause, bad husband, no-good kids, large dog and the pre-programmed responses – 'Nothing for forty minutes.'

It was warm when I arrived, the sun as sweet as honey on my skin when I woke in the mornings and lay in bed, and felt flooded with the same warm happiness, but then the winter set in, because the Middle East, particularly the coast, has a winter.

Ben Yehuda is one of the boulevards which passes from south to north; from where the Allenby Road starts and makes a sudden dive down to the sea, climbs up along the coast until it reaches North Tel Aviv where the rich people who make their money from Intel or the diamond bourse live. Eliezer ben Yehuda, after whom the street was named, is my favourite Zionist. He unilaterally decided that he was going to revive Hebrew as a spoken language and in 1881, stepped off the boat onto the soil of Jaffa and attempted a conversation with a startled porter, who, despite several grammatical errors, was able to respond in the language of the Bible on the matter, I would guess, of luggage.

He had already held a conversation in Hebrew in a café on the Boulevard Montmartre in Paris so Eliezer knew it could be done. He set himself the task of bringing up a son who would be the first person since biblical times to have Hebrew as a native language and mother tongue, necessitating the hurried coining of words suitable for the everyday life of a child, such as doll, ice cream, jelly, omelette, handkerchief, towel and bicycle. The grandson of this boy is a gay chef who for some years had his own cookery show on Israeli tv.

The block of Ben Yehuda between Gordon and Mapu contained almost everything I needed to sustain life, apart from a dry cleaner which was a block away, a bookstore, five minutes' walk inland, and two blocks further south a restaurant which I went to when it got really cold and craved the Ashkenazi food of my childhood – chicken soup, chopped liver and strudel.

Anchoring the block, in the centre, was an imposing synagogue to which on Friday nights and Saturday mornings nicely dressed middle-aged people walked, the men in suits, the women in dresses and hats, looking identical to the ones who strolled past my parents' house on their way to the synagogue at the end of our road in suburban Liverpool. Indeed they were exactly like my parents and all my relatives and if I erased the supermarket across the street, the Supersol, I could have been at home in 1950s England.

But the Supersol was a fact of life, a big fat fact, guarded by bearded Russians with pistols on their belts, who lounged on stools, checking shoppers with their wands, looking for explosive devices. Inside, the aisles were full of strange and also familiar goods. Whole displays of different kinds of humus, with pine nuts, and without, with *zatar*, and without. Wissotsky teas decorated with unrecognisable herbs. Breakfast cereals with pictures of cartoon animals on the packets. Half an aisle of tempting Elite chocolate (one of Israel's chief exports).

Across the street, on Friday mornings, a fattish man would play the violin, busking for shekels. The city pavements were full of classical music, performed by former members of Soviet symphony orchestras. There was all-out musical war between Mozart and the Nokia ring-tone.

On the far corner, facing Mapu, the Hagalil Homeopathic Pharmacy, established 1935 according to its sign, perhaps by German refugees suffering from the higher hypochondria, carrying with them from Berlin their precious vials of Dr Bach's rescue

remedy. The Higalil had sold me a small brown bottle of euca-
lyptus oil to put in the bath to clear out my blocked nose when,
on New Year's Eve, I came down with flu so severe that in my
delirium I imagined it was a secret weapon of the Hamas, a bio-
logical invention from the slums of the Rafah refugee camp in
Gaza, designed to defeat decisively and once and for all the
Zionist enemy.

Toy shop, travel agent, florist, several hairdressers, Italian
restaurant, ice-cream parlour, stores that sold Judaica (silver candlesticks, menorahs, spice boxes), antique map shop, two banks,
greengrocer, cheap clothes, shoe shop, Christian Bible store,
falafel take-away, convenience stores, internet access, several
cafés (three of which I frequented at different times of the
day) . . . and I must be forgetting something because I never
counted all the shops on that one block, knowing that, like the
stars, they could never be counted, you'd always miss something,
a little news stand or a seller of lottery tickets.

When the sun was hidden behind the boiling clouds, and it
was too stormy to walk along the beach, this block of Ben Yehuda
was my whole life.

I always asked people, 'Where did your family come from?'
And they always told me. The answer never came without a
story and they would tell it you at the drop of a hat. No one ever
said, 'Mind your own business!' In fact I asked an Israeli to tell
me the Hebrew for this expression and he told me the language
did not even contain the phrase. 'An Israeli minding his own
business is an oxymoron,' he said.

'I'm from Salonika,' said the taxi driver from the cab company
round the corner.

'How did your family survive the war?' I asked him.

'My parents fought with the communist partisans and for this
reason, we are always on the left in Israeli politics.'

They came from Spain, Turkey, Yemen, Syria, Poland,

Ukraine, Lithuania, Iran, Yugoslavia, France, Germany, the Benelux, Holland, Egypt, South Africa, Moldova, Siberia, Morocco, Tunisia, Algeria, Ethiopia, India, Cuba, Argentina, Mexico, Afghanistan.

The whole street was dense with the Jewish Diaspora re-meeting itself for the first time in two thousand years and saying to each other, 'Hey, remember us?'

'No.'

The further away anyone was from that block of Ben Yehuda Street, the easier it seemed to find a solution to the conflict between Israelis and Palestinians, that stubborn mess in the centre of the Middle East, and the more I studied these solutions, the more I thought that they depended for their implementation on a population of table football men, painted in the colours of the two teams: blue and white for the Israelis, black, white, green and red for the Palestinians. All the international community had to do was to twist the levers and the little players would kick and swing and send the ball into the net, to victory.

The supporters of each side, the fan base, impassioned and single-minded, had turned the protagonists in this tragedy into receptacles for slogans, never bothering to imagine that the 'Arab terrorists' or the 'Zionist colonialists' were living, breathing human beings. They were not wood but flesh and blood, and they carried inside their heads not only their history, their grievances, their fears and anxieties but a complicated network of culture, language, religion, sense of humour. It was the same in Israel as it was in Palestine. And this was what most offended me, the dehumanisation. The belief that life could ever be tidy and that people could be stacked up on the shelf, like teas or cereal. I was sickened by it.

I was in Tel Aviv, not Ramallah, but I was certain that there was a block of a street there on which I could have spent an

equal amount of time, and arrived, eventually, at the same conclusion.

When I put aside my novel, I still had something to say, or
something I felt had to be said, even by me, who was not an
Israeli or a political analyst or an activist or someone with an
angry polemic boiling inside me.

I knew I would get the Israelis wrong, that in thinking I could
know them I was guilty of the same *chutzpah* as all those political
theorists. I wasn't a prophet or a messiah or zealot. I was trying to
understand the Jews, that vexed, contradictory question that
had plagued me all my life, and the Jews I was trying to understand were the ones who intensely inhabited a coastal plain in
the middle of the Levant, making a mess for which there seemed
to be no solution.

Or if I was really honest, I would say that I was there in Tel
Aviv because I like it. I don't know why, I just do. It is the only
city I know (apart from the one inside my head, the one that *I*
built), which does not make me long to head for the airport to
find another place, out of dissatisfaction, boredom and commonplace curiosity for what's next.

Sopher

I have made many journeys to Israel in recent years but the first, when I was sixteen, took place in the summer of 1967. My best friend Sara and I, chafing against bourgeois life in the Liverpool suburbs, desperate to meet boys and kiss them, wanted to go on holiday without our parents. There was only one country in the world to which they would even consider allowing their pampered princesses to travel alone, and that was Israel, because 'you're among family', they said. Not literally, since we didn't have any Israeli relatives. They meant that the whole of the Jewish people should be considered family, and could be relied on to look after two nice Jewish girls alone abroad, because that was what you would do yourself.

   The fact that the Six Day War was barely over, when we took off in an Air France plane at the beginning of July 1967, did not bother them. We had been signed up to a youth programme, advertised at the back of the *Jewish Chronicle*, which offered a summer in Israel to eager Diaspora teens, with lectures, language courses, tours of archaeological sites, a week on a kibbutz – the full Zionist indoctrination, which, reading between the lines, we could see all boiled down to one thing: boys, and the opportunities to kiss them.

On our arrival in Israel, with £25 pocket money each to last two months, the maximum you could take out of the country during those times of British currency restrictions, we dutifully went to the post office and sent telegrams home to confirm our safe arrival and made our way to Haifa where we were to meet the rest of the party. And waited and waited, because they didn't turn up, and to this day I have no idea whether we were in the wrong place, or our parents had been ripped off, or all those other teenagers, including the boys with the kissable lips, had thought better of the whole enterprise, given the recent warfare. Never mind that the Egyptian air force had just been annihilated, when it came to Jewish princesses unchaperoned abroad, you could never get too hysterically anxious.

We walked up a flight of steps to a small office containing a branch of the Jewish Agency which dealt with arriving immigrants and received the brush-off. Two pathetic teenage girls were of no interest to them.

We stumbled out onto the hot, cruel streets, crying our eyes out, alone and frightened. And then an old man of, oh, he must have been at least thirty, came over to Sara and put his arm round her. I thought, that's all we need, some ancient bloke harassing us. But he was not a stranger, he was her cousin.

Her father, dissatisfied with the tour arrangements, had rung the kibbutz where his nephew was working as a volunteer, helping out in the fields while the kibbutz boys were still mobilised to their reserve units. He demanded that the kibbutz secretary go and get Morrie and bring him to the phone. Then he ordered him to get a bus south to Haifa and walk the streets until he found his cousin. Which he did, proving, triumphantly, to our parents, that they had been right all along, that in Israel you were among family and that nothing bad could ever happen to you.

No one could track down the rest of the tour group. Morrie took us north to the kibbutz, Ein Gev, on the edge of the Sea of Galilee, under the newly occupied Golan Heights, where we failed to kiss any kibbutz boys, partly because there were so few around, and partly because the kibbutz girls would have killed us if we pathetic specimens of Diaspora humanity had dared even to look at one of their men. I did kiss some South Africans, who delivered first-hand accounts of the apartheid system. Some were refusing to return home, determined to stay on in the great Jewish socialist experiment. After we left at the end of the summer, a few of them were expelled from the kibbutz for smoking hash.

I came home having learned to swim and learned to smoke, addicted to cheap gaspers which were given out free every week, an allowance of a pack a day. I met Palestinians and found them charming. I got lost in the Orthodox quarter of Jerusalem and, bare-armed, was stoned by small children from the windows of some houses. I saw the Wailing Wall, the most (indeed arguably the only) Jewish holy site, a few weeks after its liberation from Jordan. I danced in a nightclub with a paratrooper in uniform, who bashed his feet against the floor in his big boots. 'My best friend was killed,' he said, as he tried to grab my breasts. What could I say? I knew absolutely nothing about anything. I was like an amoeba compared with him. I had to let him grab. On the kibbutz I had lain on the beach and the Israeli girls my own age pointed up at the Golan, right above us. 'Until we took that territory,' they said, 'Syrian snipers used to try to shoot us while we were swimming.'

At the end of the summer I came home, went back to school and forgot about Israel for a long time.

I did not return until March 1998, thirty-one years later. In that long hiatus I had had a number of differences of opinion with my parents about Israel and about Zionism. I started by refusing to 'come out' at the Blue and White Ball at the Adelphi Hotel in Liverpool, where Jewish girls in white dresses with blue sashes across their budding chests were 'presented' against a backdrop of the Israeli flag to the Lord Mayor, who happened to be Jewish, and the orchestra played 'Hatikva', the Israeli national anthem, and then we all went looking for someone to press those chests against and give us trophy love bites. I can't say I rejected this event out of ideological conviction, more a gut feeling that in 1968 there were better things to do than be a Jewish debutante, and these involved secretly getting a prescription for the pill and decoding the drug references in the Beatles' 'Lucy in the Sky with Diamonds'.

I'm not embarrassed by this vacuousness. I was only a teenager. I am more embarrassed by some of the things I said later, to my father.

My parents were unfamiliar with political theories; they didn't know anything about imperialism, colonialism, pan-Arabism, post-colonialism, hegemony or any other isms, ists and onies apart from anti-Semitism and fascism. The first, for them, was an enduring state of affairs which could be held back, temporarily, by the dam of Jewish willpower, but was sure to come gushing out when you least expected it. The second had been defeated by the military might of those great powers, Britain, America, and the Soviet Union, whose leader, Stalin, they had a soft spot for, not because they were communists, but because they admired the fighting spirit of the Red Army and the huge losses it had had to take in order to roll back the Nazi advance on Moscow.

They were British, but not; eastern European, but not. They used Yiddish as a secret language to conceal what they thought was too important to be endured by their children: business failures, money worries, shocking family gossip concerning adultery and homosexuality, but not what the world would like to do to the Jews if only it got half a chance, information they felt we were never too young to learn, digest, and which would assist us in forming an opinion. And this consisted of staying inside the confines of family and community where you were safe, because outside it there was nothing but hatred and persecution, and they knew this directly from their own experience because in 1947 there were anti-Semitic riots in Liverpool in response to the kidnapping and murder by the Irgun of two British sergeants in Palestine.

Israel for them was a flag, a national anthem, pride. Above all, I think, pride, the antidote to humiliation.

Maybe it was around the time of the PLO hijackings that I first heard about anti-Zionism and the glamour of the freedom fighters, those angry-eyed girl heroines, like the revolutionary and plane hijacker Leila Khaled (today a housewife in suburban Amman). And when I did, I knew that at long last I had a sharpened weapon in the endless war I was fighting against my father – his authority, his physical size, the way he ate his food with his mouth open, the way he ordered my mother around, his selfishness and sentimentality and everything about him that was in me and which I wished to cut out, with a knife if necessary. It was a war against his idea that a daughter does not leave her parents' home unless she is a prostitute; against the God who had wilfully not given him the sons he wanted, the sons who should have inherited his business and carried on his name; against his interminable stories, of the years he spent in America in the Roaring Twenties; against his business with its smells of chemicals roused in vats to become hair dye, perm and setting lotion.

My anti-Zionism was a form of cruelty and abuse which had nothing at all to do with any Palestinians I had ever met, because of course apart from those very brief encounters in Israel, I never had met any. It was sound and fury: cheap, fake Sixties ideology, choosing those arguments that would hurt my father most. My phoney empathy with the Palestinians was a failure of empathy for my parents. I did not acknowledge their reality during the war: the blitz, in which they were crowded on air-raid shelter benches as the Nazi planes flew overhead; the terrible fear of invasion and its consequences; the day the war in Europe ended, my mother with a fiancé dead somewhere in the Pacific and a brother in a military cemetery in Italy, was dancing on the steps of St George's Hall as the cold spring wind blew across the Atlantic; then my newly married parents, waiting for me, waiting for me to be conceived and born, in their honeymoon flat on Linnet Lane, holding hands as they listened on the wireless to the news from New York where the United Nations was voting on whether or not to give the Jews a country, and their joy, their *exultation*, the idea that the world had done something right for a change (but not their own government, which abstained, and made them even more not British than they were already).

I had what they didn't: an ology and an ism, and was an ist. I knew that their sentimental visions of Israel were mostly rubbish, the empty, lying slogans: the 'land without people for a people without land'; the heroism of 'our' soldiers, 'the most moral army in the world', which had massacred civilians in the village of Deir Yassin. Even the trees we had saved so hard to plant would later prove to be the wrong kind of trees, leaching water from the dry soil, eroding the earth. I knew everything and they knew nothing. I was an ist, which was greater and more universal than their provincial Jewish ish.

The Israeli invasion of Lebanon, 1982, a year before my father died of emphysema, his body starved, like a doll in the bed. I walked towards the demonstration at which we ists would pace up and down with our placards. Approaching, I saw a young man unfurl a banner in which the Nazi swastika was joined (by this sign: =) to a Jewish star of David. A few feet from the demonstration, I turned round and saw a bus which was just closing its doors and I leapt onto it and never went back to any anti-Zionist demonstrations or paid any attention either to anti or pro Zionism. I wasn't interested, I didn't want to know. Beirut, the second intifada, the Oslo agreement, the return of the PLO from exile, the assassination of the Israeli prime minister Yitzhak Rabin – I would mute the tv when these items reached the news because resolving the political and emotional knots inside me was too unbearable. I didn't have the strength.

Only when I was writing a book about my parents, about the progressive loss of memory that devastated my mother's brain, taking down with it the family history and hence ourselves, did my own mind turn again to that country which I had used to cause my father so much grief, which had nothing to do, in those vicious arguments, with a real place or real people, except in that they were shadows, outlines to be filled in with what we brought to them from our own unspent needs and urges.

It was in 1997, over a decade after his death, during the fiftieth anniversary of Indian independence, watching the tv coverage, that I remembered that in a year's time it would be the fiftieth anniversary of the birth of Israel. And I thought, for the first time, of my parents, newly married, having survived the Liverpool blitz – noting the letters that had come from uncles and cousins in Kiev, a correspondence that had been maintained with punctual regularity up till 1939, then stopped dead, nothing more heard from them – listening to the radio with the news that the Jews were to have their own country. And my heart went out to them; an act of imaginative empathy for what they must have been feeling, that the pogroms, the oppression, the genocide were finally coming to an end. It finishes *here*. They did not know from colonialism, they never once considered the Arab case. They were incapable of thinking from the point of view of the Other. And it was my decision, after years and years of hostility which eventually tempered into cold indifference to Israel, to try for the first time to see things from my own parents' perspective, which is a feat one is normally only capable of when one reaches middle age.

I went to Israel to write about the fiftieth anniversary for the *Guardian*. It was my idea, I wanted to go. My subject was the vexing question, what is a Jew? The photographer who had been assigned to come with me had to drop out at the last minute after a terrible family crisis. For two days I wandered round Tel Aviv on my own with nothing to do and no one to talk to because I didn't know anybody. I looked at the buildings, the dilapidated, dun-coloured apartments, and thought I'd never seen an uglier city, until slowly I began to notice its extraordinary features: the curved corners jutting out into the street, like a ship at sea, the rounded balconies. And I, who knew little or nothing about architecture, abruptly understood what I was looking at: the Bauhaus.

There were two responses: first, I was mad to know who had built them and who had been their earliest inhabitants; second, I saw them as a metaphor for the Zionist idealists, my parents included, who had made this place, and if it now was almost in rack and ruin, then was this not true of all idealism, eventually? I had fallen for the romance of communism, with all its flaws and its descent into terror, show trials and mass murder, so I could easily see from the point of view of its progenitors the romance of Zionism, particularly when it came to those Russian revolutionaries who arrived in Palestine and in 1909 decided to build a city on the sand dunes of the eastern Mediterranean, the first Jewish city since biblical times. Even if there was someone else there already.

I could not have been more fortunate in the person who was sent out to replace the absent photographer, when he finally arrived on an overnight flight. We had breakfast together and I asked him if he had been to Israel before. What a question.

His name was Judah Passow and the Passow family were part of the history of Zionism, part of its proudest history, part indeed of what would enter the national consciousness. His father, a young American rabbi, met his future wife at a Haganah meeting in Washington during the Second World War, and in 1947 they were sent to Europe to find concentration camp survivors to load onto the illegal immigrant ship, the *Exodus*, which, when turned back at Haifa harbour and forced by the British authorities to return to Europe, would precipitate world-wide sympathy and support for the creation by the United Nations of a Jewish state. The Passows stayed on in Israel and their eldest son, Judah, was born in Holon in January 1949, conceived there just before the founding of the state. The family returned to America in the 1950s, but in 1971, as a student radical refusing the Vietnam draft, Judah came back to Israel where he served in the army during the Yom Kippur War in one of its most savage battles in the Sinai desert, and was among the first six soldiers to cross the Suez Canal to beat back an Egyptian battery on the other side.

He became a photojournalist, covering the Russian invasion of Afghanistan, the wars in Lebanon and Bosnia, the first intifada. His parents had wanted to bring into the world one of the first Israelis, and they succeeded in that they had somehow managed to remove from his DNA Diaspora neurosis, or perhaps it was the war that made him tough and warm and funny and stoical, just as at home taking pictures of children playing in the rubble of a destroyed house in a Palestinian refugee camp as he was going out with an platoon of Israeli soldiers to arrest a ticking bomb in Nablus.

His photographs, spare, uncluttered, powerfully constructed, hang on my wall at home: an Italian medical team operating on the body of an injured boy in a Beirut field hospital, composed like an old master, and nothing has ever conveyed to me quite so well the sorrow and the pity of war.

Over the next few days we travelled the country together, and talked and talked, and I saw it through his eyes: highly critical, scathing about the corruption, cruelty, injustice (particularly towards its Arab minority), but neither Zionism nor Israel was an idea that you argued about. He couldn't care less about ideologues. It was, for him, the place where he was born, and which he identified as his nationality. He must have stood on every metre of its soil. He also knew the West Bank and Gaza almost as intimately; he was clear-eyed about the occupation and about the army in which he had served, about the necessity to defend the country and the immorality of its incursions against the civilian Palestinian population.

He took me to meet his parents in their apartment in Jerusalem where his father, at the age of eighty-five, was still teaching courses at the Hebrew University.

And out of that meeting, perhaps – talking to them about the Tel Aviv they remembered from the 1940s when they were young, the Tel Aviv that was known then as the White City, sparkling white – came the novel I would begin writing on my return, *When I Lived in Modern Times*, set in Tel Aviv in 1946. When it was published, in March 2000, I thought I had been making a portrait of the beginning of a period of history that was just about to come to an end; that by the autumn there was to be a Palestinian state, and the long war between Jews and Arabs would be over. It was a wildly misguided reading of political events, which people still pore over in order to assign blame. But it is also a novel about a city, and about my own relationship with it.

I made a number of short visits during the writing of the book, none longer than ten days. With each one, I met a few more people, and then I began to know quite a lot of people. They were not selected in order to represent a cross-section of the population, they were just people I met, usually through someone else, the obvious chain of how one makes acquaintances anywhere. There was a long gap after February 2000. When the intifada started in the autumn of that year, after the failure of talks at Camp David, I was very busy with another novel, and anyway I was scared of the suicide bombs.

In April 2003, in the middle of the Iraq war, I returned. I was homesick for the place and tired of London and its debates about the Iraq war which could not be stopped because it had already started. I began to write the novel there that would prove to be so problematic, and decided it was time that I became more than a fleeting guest. I definitely did not want to come as a reporter, one of the crowd that hung out at the American Colony hotel in East Jerusalem, who stuck together, who saw themselves as a roving pack of witnesses to war and to horror. I wanted to watch Israel, I wanted to try to understand what it felt like to be part of it.

In July I made another trip to find an apartment. In October I arrived; I left at the end of January 2004. Later that year, in the autumn, I returned again, to spend a week with the Gaza settlers. And in February 2005 I came back, this time with my friend the Palestinian writer Samir el Youssef.

This is the story of these journeys. But I reiterate, I went there as a *sopher*, a writer, not as a political analyst, and each of these professions, I think, has its own very different rules of engagement. I did not come to witness, to make a statement, or sign a petition. I didn't meet, intentionally, any politicians, or generals, or heads of NGOs, or activists. I tried to wriggle out of invitations to attend meetings or press briefings. I didn't conduct any interviews. I just spent a lot of time sitting in cafés, listening, drinking my cup of coffee, while the country assembled itself around me, in all its perplexing reality.

Chutzpah

A few doors down from the Supersol supermarket on Ben Yehuda Street, a small bookstore sold Testaments, new and old, carved doves made of olive wood, crosses, biblical commentary, gifts and knick-knacks. The store kept good opening hours but there was rarely anyone in there. It was a Christian outpost in a Jewish neighbourhood and the only people I ever saw browsing were Filipinos: care workers and home helps imported from abroad, slim girls in white uniforms and white shoes, their hair tied back in long black ponytails, guiding old people home like pilot boats bringing a crippled ship in to land.

Across the street were a number of silversmiths who made and sold jewellery and Judaica: candlesticks, menorahs, spice boxes, seder plates. Their clientele were the tourists from the concrete boxes that lined the shore; the rich Americans would cross the heavy traffic on HaYarkon Street and walk up Gordon or Mapu on their way to the cafés of Dizengoff Street until they hit Ben Yehuda and would stop and spend hundreds of dollars on genuine solid silver *chatchkes* to adorn their dining-room table, or keep locked in a glass-fronted case.

But there weren't any American tourists. There were French tourists, lots of them. For the years of the intifada they were more or less single-handedly keeping the tourist economy going, and when I went with my future landlady, Yael, to view her apartment on Ruppin Street she told me I was the first non-French applicant she had received in three years. The Jews were leaving France. It was impossible for a Jew to live there any more, they said. They were being beaten and spat at, their synagogues desecrated. The French government did its best but couldn't help, the hate came from the streets. A small chic fromagerie appeared on Basel Street to cater for their cultivated tastes.

I was quite upset to pass the empty silver stores every day. The windows were choked with beautiful things and nobody was buying them, so one day, just before Chanukah, I went in and bought a silver filigree menorah in the Yemenite style, the Jews from Yemen being masters of silver ornamentation.

I lit my eight coloured candles, one for each day, in commemoration of the David and Goliath fight between the Maccabees and the Greeks. The Maccabees triumphed in 165 BC and reclaimed the Temple, where they found, when they wanted to rededicate it, that there wasn't enough oil to light the holy lamp, but by a miracle one bottle of oil lasted eight nights. Nice little story. The streets filled with people peddling sugar doughnuts, because in Israel, the eating of fried foods at Chanukah in remembrance of the oil had come to mean deep-fried dough balls dredged in sugar. There were menorahs everywhere you went, in every bar and restaurant and shop, as ubiquitous as Christmas trees in Britain.

In a taxi, returning from Herzlyia, the driver turned on his radio to the dispatch office and through the tinny speakers a voice came, singing the Chanukah song:

> Hanerot halalu anachnu madlikim
> Al hanissim ve' al haniflaot
> Al hatshu-ot ve' al hamilchamot
> She-asita la' avoteynu
> Bayamim hahem, bazman hazeh
> Al yedey kohanecha hakdoshim.

> We light these candles
> For the miracles and the wonders
> For the redemption and the battles
> That you made for our forefathers
> In those days at this season
> Through your holy priests.

The driver joined in. 'Sing,' he said to me. I didn't know if it was an invitation or an order. Someone once remarked that Israel is the only country in the world where 'Excuse me' can sound like a threat. I sang.

I am not religious. I am, in the words of a rabbi I know, 'tone deaf to the divine'. So I did not decide one day to go to the shop near the Supersol to buy a Bible because I was in the Holy Land, the land that God Almighty gave to my forefathers in the covenant he made with Abraham, clearly laid out in perhaps the world's first recorded real estate deal:

> And I will give unto thee, and to thy seed after thee, the land wherein thou art a stranger, all the land of Canaan, for an everlasting possession; and I will be their God. (Genesis 17:8)

It was interesting to see it there in black and white, but what led me to the Torah (the first five books of the Old Testament) was reading the autobiography of the Nobel physicist Richard Feynman, who explained that when he looked at nature he felt a sense of awe because he understood that it was governed by a set of unitary laws, it was not random. In the same way, Judaism's great message, monotheism, laid down a set of principles that governed the whole of creation, not just the part in which it originated with its petty local gods.

The first law of Judaism is the 'Shema', the first prayer and the last, the one said on waking and the one said with your dying breath: 'Hear O Israel, the lord thy God, the lord is One.' This is the fundamental disagreement Judaism has with Christianity: God cannot be divided into three.

Physics led me to the Bible; I wanted to know if God could be a metaphor for the Big Bang theory.

Most cultures and societies inhabit space: the land to which they have attached themselves. In each country there is a word or phrase which conveys the complex feelings of the people for their spot on the earth; in German it is *Heimat*, meaning home or homeland, but also the sense of the place you lived when you were a child, the origins of yourself. We can speak, easily, I think, of something called 'English soil', meaning that it has certain physical characteristics and is distinguished by particular types of vegetation, such as oak trees and dandelions. I can usually tell when looking at a picture of a landscape – a photograph in a magazine or a painting in the National Gallery – that this is England not Italy or America, despite the fact that as an entirely urban entity I can't recognise, let alone name, anything that grows on it. Despite the millennia of wandering, Judaism also contains a sense of place, but in a kind of negative equation, the longing for a return from exile: 'By the waters of Babylon I lay down and yea I wept when I remembered Zion.'

At each Passover the ritual words are spoken: 'Next year in Jerusalem.' For centuries this promise operated as a metaphor of an ideal that one should strive to attain, of a spiritual return. The Zionism that emerged at the end of the nineteenth century after the Hungarian-born journalist Theodor Herzl reported on the Dreyfus trial in France (the anti-Semitic witch-hunt of a Jewish officer) and wrote his book *Judenstaat* (Jewish state) took the idea of return literally. In 1999, when the transvestite singer Dana International won the Eurovision Song Contest, under whose rules next year's contest is held in the home capital of this year's winner, banners rose up from the audience: 'Next year in Jerusalem!'

For a Palestinian, the soil of Palestine was Arab and always would be. The state that had grown up on it was alien and full of aliens, as unwelcome as that import to Britain from America, the grey squirrel, which has now conquered and almost driven to extinction its indigenous relative, the more attractive red squirrel.

Despite God's gift to his chosen people of the land of Canaan, Jews are a people not of space, but of time. Ours is the God of history. 'Remember' is his most important injunction.

It does not surprise me that Jews in the twentieth century took so eagerly to the novel form, for to be a Jew is to be in permanent possession of a very long story filled with incredible characters, battle scenes, kings, preachers, scarlet women, madmen, fools. The critic George Steiner wrote of Jewish scholarship thus: 'The text is home, each commentary a return.'

The nature of memory is key to understanding Jewishness, and hence Israeliness. The enormous importance Jews place on graves and cemeteries is nothing to do with a death cult, or ancestor worship, but an insistence on the chain of generations.

Leaving the dead behind in their wanderings was a great trauma. When the government was planning the evacuation of Jewish settlers from Gaza, one of the things they had to discuss was how to move the graves as well. The army had a code of ethics which did not allow it to leave the fallen on the battlefield; every attempt was made to reclaim the bodies and return them home for a proper burial. While I was in Israel I watched a remarkable ceremony on tv. The government had exchanged several hundred Lebanese prisoners for four coffins containing the corpses of three Jewish and one Druze soldier. The bodies arrived at the airport where a tarmac commemoration was enacted. The prime minister Ariel Sharon tried and failed to bow at the waist, and instead lowered his head in front of each wooden box, including that of the Druze soldier, whose parents were comforted by their *uqql*. Some people thought it was a bad exchange, but Sharon was adamant. We do this, he said, because of the importance we attach to Jewish burial.

This chain of life, this sense of a continuous relationship with the past which is forged by the repeating of the story and by the examination of the story's meanings through Talmudic scholarship (possibly the first literary criticism), this enactment of one's Jewishness as opposed to adherence to a belief system, has shaped the way Jews see the world.

There is a well-known joke about the essence of all Jewish festivals: 'They tried to kill us, we survived, let's eat.' When at the Passover seder table in the mid-1960s my father delivered his annual impromptu sermon, the act of a man who adored the sound of his own voice, he ranged across the events that were taking place on the news – the assassination of the South African prime minister Verwoerd, the civil rights movement in America and the suffering Irish just across the water – and reminded us that once we were slaves in the land of Egypt, and when he said us, he did not mean the Jews, as a Christian might speak of Christians, fellow-believers, but, we were to understand, people a few generations back from my grandparents.

This *we* was taken very personally, to include the individuals sitting round the table. We had been the victims of genocide, twenty years before. We had been beaten and abused by the Cossacks sixty years ago. We were thrown out of Spain five hundred years ago. We defied the Romans at Masada two thousand years ago. We were exiles in Babylon three thousand years ago. We were being threatened by Abdul Nasser, President of Egypt, right now.

The Bible was the family history. The exodus, the parting of the Red Sea, the wandering in the desert, the ascent to receive the Ten Commandments, Moses' fatal slip-up when he failed to follow God's instructions to the letter and was allowed to see, but not enter, the Promised Land – this was our story, carried from century to century, land to land. I have a CD of music composed in the time of Columbus' discovery of America, the same year as the Jews were expelled from Spain, in which the medieval voices are still commemorating, in Ladino (the language of Sephardic Iberia), that expulsion, and the recording includes a reproduction of the splashing of the sea's waves, held back by God's hand.

For many years I had only occasionally looked at the Bible, and even then just for the beauty of the translation in the English King James version, its seventeenth-century prose contemporary with that of Shakespeare and John Donne. The novelist David Grossman told me he was horrified by it. It gave no sense at all of the granite quality of the original language, as if the opening words of Genesis were hewn out of the rock of the planet itself. Nonetheless, I could not make myself part from this synthesis between the language of my forefathers and the only language I speak, and the one in which I write.

In the apartment on Ruppin Street I sat down to reread the story, as told from the pulpits of English churches, that was also the lodestone of the Jewish religion and of Jewish identity, and was brought up short at chapter 32, which contained, in a few verses, an extraordinary account of a dispute between Moses and God. It had nothing to do with Feynman's sense of awe at the coherence of the physical universe, but it did shine a sudden shaft of light into Jewish identity.

Moses is up on the mountain receiving the ten commandments, and also receiving a whole set of specific instructions about how to build a tabernacle in compliance with divine building regulations ('ten cubits shall be the length of a board, and a cubit and a half shall be the breadth of a board'); meanwhile, down below, the children of Israel have decided that they don't know what Moses is up to on Mount Sinai, but he's been gone a really long time. How are they to comprehend that he is committing to memory the entire social code for civilisation? His younger brother, Aaron, can see that they are getting restless, so he says, 'Okay, go and make a graven idol; in fact, get your wives to give you their gold earrings and I'll melt them down and make us a nice gold calf to worship.' The children of Israel organise the burnt offerings, have a meal and then take their clothes off and settle down to enjoy themselves, as you do when you have been hanging around a long time and are feeling in need of some rest and recreation.

You think God doesn't notice? He goes ballistic. Look at them, thanking a gold bovine for bringing them out of the land of Egypt when *I* did it, me. 'I have seen these people,' he says to Moses, 'and they are a stiff-necked people. Now therefore let me alone, that my wrath wax hot against them.'

What happens next is perhaps the greatest event that has ever occurred in any religion.

Moses begins to argue back. 'Listen,' he says, 'first of all, how's this going to look to the Egyptians? You told everyone that the Jews were your chosen people, you brought us out of Egypt, and then you turn round and slay the lot of us. Second, you made a promise, you told Abraham, Isaac and Jacob that you were going to multiply our seed as the stars of the sky and that we were going to get the land of Canaan forever. We've got a contract. So *turn from thy fierce wrath, and repent of this evil against thy people.'*

I could not believe it. A man stands alone on a mountain and tells the creator of the universe to repent. He accuses the Lord of Everything There Is, of harbouring bad thoughts, of being, dare one say it, flawed. And in that sense, human.

God listens, he thinks about it. Okay, he says, I repent.

After Moses has come down from the mountain, God kills three thousand of his chosen people, just to set an example. But he promises that he'll make good on his word, the land is theirs, he'll send an angel on ahead to drive out the Canaanites, the Amorites, the Hittites and several other ites. They're getting a land flowing with milk and honey, but what they're not getting is an actual sight of the deity. Only Moses, inside the newly built tabernacle, sees God face to face, 'as a man speaketh to his friend'.

God will not reveal himself to his people because he doesn't seem to like them. 'I will not go up in the midst of thee; for thou art a stiff-necked people,' he says, using the phrase stiff-necked a second time. Then a few lines later a third time as he instructs Moses to tell the children of Israel what his problem with them is: 'Ye are a stiff-necked people.'

It occurred to me that one of the most marked characteristics of Zionism is the range of adherence and opposition to it, so you can find Israelis who believe that God promised them the land fair and square and that the Palestinians and Palestinian citizens of Israel should be forcibly expelled to Jordan, and other Israelis who believe equally forcibly that Israel is an illegitimate state, created out of collusion with the Nazis. Because if you come from a people whose leading prophet was prepared to face down God himself, then clearly anything is possible.

This quality of argumentativeness, of a stubborn, almost principled tendency to do the opposite of what others might see as being in your own interests, of non-conformism, of being a perpetual awkward squad, always in the wrong place at the wrong time, became my own form of guidance during my time in Israel. And later on, I would find out that there was even a word for it, which would make life a whole lot easier when I understood what it was. But for a long time I was totally in the dark.

Balagan

Winter. I have been in the apartment on Ruppin Street for six weeks.

Outside, howling gales, thunder, lightning. The sea is a monstrosity, the beach restaurants are abandoned and overwhelmed. These nights I can't sleep because of the crash of buildings falling to bits, a washing line collapsing, a corner of masonry crumbling and taking with it the telephone wires. Plastic garbage cans roll along the pavements, palm trees shudder and their leaves like swords cut me in the face as I walk home through the shuddering wind. Oleander and hibiscus bushes shed their flowers; in the morning the garden is bloody with bruised petals. This usually continues for three days and nights then the storm abates, the sun comes out, the skies are blue and the air warm and you forget all about the winter, until you wake up a few days later to the sound of renewed violence, more rain, more thunder. Then summer, which in its own way is equally unbearable.

On the evening of 10 December 2003, after a telephone conversation with J., who had told me some confidential information that the prime minister, Ariel Sharon, had decided to unilaterally pull out of some of the occupied territories, as long as they can talk the Americans into it, who at this stage would need some persuading, he said, I felt cold and went into the bathroom to turn on the taps. I noticed that the plug, which didn't come with a chain or any other means of attachment, had fallen behind the washing machine, situated in the bathroom because the narrow kitchen can't house too many appliances.

I stood on tiptoe, leaned across the bath and reached behind the washing machine to pick up the plug, and as I did so, my foot slipped on the bathmat, and to my amazement I found myself lying face-down inside the tub, my limbs thrashing, like a starfish.

In the moment of impact my glasses had flown across the room, and though I could see, things lacked focus. There was just the general idea of the surface of the bath, the indignity of my position, and a feeling of wetness which I did not understand because I hadn't turned on the taps.

It is harder than it looks to pick yourself up out of a bath in which you are lying face-down when the sides are slippery and you haven't anything to hold on to and are wet and getting wetter. My face was becoming submerged in the rapidly filling bath and I had to stretch back my neck to keep my nose out of the puddle that was getting bigger. And it suddenly became apparent that it was actually possible to drown in a few inches of bathwater, which I had always thought was an urban myth.

I have always had a neurotic paranoia about the fragility of life; that I could accidentally look the wrong way while crossing the road, or be distracted and fall down a hole, or slip on an icy pavement and break my spine in the wrong place. Mountaineers and potholers, round-the-world yachtswomen, anyone who leaves the house to undertake an unnecessary journey just for the sake of it, are asking for trouble. I get this from my parents who had recoiled from the horrors of everyday life – playground swings, swimming pools – and let out the ancient primal cry of their race: 'It's dangerous!'

So this is it. Death by misadventure, drowning in a bathtub in a rented apartment in Tel Aviv, while reaching for a rubber plug. The end of the story, only 36 pages in.

But dying isn't my thing. I have an underdeveloped death wish. By contorting my body and using all the strength of my arms, I managed to get myself to a kneeling position and step out of the bathtub and hence saved my own life, which I had always wanted to do since I nearly choked to death on a piece of steak in a restaurant in London and the maître d' lunged at me and did the Heimlich manoeuvre. When I got home I looked it up on the internet and learned how to do it when alone, using the back of a chair.

The floor was awash with water and I didn't know why. After a few minutes I found my glasses, which had skittered across the room into the shower stall.

I put the glasses on and looked around and noticed that on the wall where the cheap plastic taps had been were two large holes like an elephant's nostrils, gushing cataracts of water. In the moment of impact when I fell into the bath I suppose I must have reached out to grab the taps with the hose shower attachment, and under the weight of my descent they had detached from the wall.

I picked up the taps and tried to reattach them but they were irrevocably broken. The cement that had held them in was soaked and crumbling. I couldn't think of a single solution to the problem, which didn't surprise me because I am not of a practical disposition. I could count on myself to talk my way out of any situation, but anything that requires the use of hands or tools or logistical thinking I pay someone else to do.

This horrible accident, the flood that was engulfing the bathroom, meant that I would have to ring my landlady, the terrifying Yael, who walked like a panther through the city and stared at me with gimlet eyes.

'You have to turn off the stopcock,' she said.

'Yes, thank god, what an easy solution. Where is it?'

'I don't know. I ring Rafi, my plumber. Stay there.'

I waited for a few more minutes while the water took a look out of the bathroom door and began to roll across the wooden floor of the living room, heading towards the cane furniture.

A few minutes later Yael arrived with a young man, nicely dressed.

She shouted orders at him in Hebrew. He went to the kitchen and moved the refrigerator, she gave him more orders, he reached round, and suddenly the sound of the waterfall, the cascade, the Niagara Falls, stopped. The water dribbled to a halt against the wall.

'Is he going to fix it?'

'That's not Rafi, he's not a plumber.'

'Who is he?'

'Just some boy who was going out for the evening that I met in the hall. You expect me to move a refrigerator?' She was sixty-five but I had thought that she could push back the sea if she'd had the interest; she was a very determined woman who made me sign a contract and negotiated a rent for the apartment a third higher than that which had been originally advertised.

'Rafi is coming tomorrow, now tell me what happened.'

I explained to her the accident.

'What a *balagan*,' she said looking at me in a rather unfavourable way. 'And you, I'm starting to think, are a *balaganiste*.'

I had already been ten days late in arriving to rent the apartment because of a disaster in London with some dental work.

What is a *balagan*? A *balagan* is a mess. If I spill a bag of sugar, I make a mess. If I am eating a hot dog and get mustard round my mouth, that is a mess. If I am too lazy to tidy up, I wind up with a mess. My desk is a mess.

But a *balagan* is more than a mess. A *balagan* is a mess that verges on the uncontrollable. It is chaos, disorder, the throwing up of your hands, because what the hell can you or anybody do about this *balagan*? Can it ever be made to bend under the rules of logic? You feel helpless, you feel overwhelmed, but sometimes the state of everything being a *balagan* becomes so normal that you start to fear and distrust the harmony of its opposite.

Yael, whom I had come to think of as the DNA of the country, surprised me by smiling. Obviously she was right at home inside the very soul of the *balagan*.

I stayed up late, drying the floors. In England we have mops with sponges at the end and a lever to squeeze out the water. In Israel there are long poles with a rubber strip and you wrap a floor cloth to the end of them. They are called a *Sponjah*, a relic from the mandate days, when the British brought here a thing called a Sponge Up which no one could pronounce.* I mopped for an

---

*Of all the disputes among early readers of this MS, none, not even the location of the American Patriot missile battery during the Gulf War (was it on top of the rubbish tip or in a field just behind it? Eyewitness accounts differ, and it has been suggested that one should take into account the *height* of the rubbish tip in 1991), has generated so much disagreement as the matter of the mop. One correspondent writes: 'If I may be a nudnig: sponga is the act of washing the floor. The device is referred to as a spongador, or more often, magav. The magav which my friend Roy brought for me from Israel is one of my dearest possessions.' Faced with refutation

hour and eventually everything dried out. The storm abated too. The morning came, and it was hot again.

'Rafi is coming at 10 o'clock,' Yael said. 'He is a very good plumber, I'm lucky to have him. You know how we met? He lost his wallet at the airport and my daughter found it and called him and since then he's always done everything for her. This is her apartment so he knows it very well. I want you to wait, and I'll press the bell downstairs and tell you when he's here, then we'll come up and you'll let us in.'

She rang the bell and I waited, and went on waiting, hovering at the door. I couldn't work out how it could take so long to climb three flights of stairs, unless Rafi had some special equipment that had to be schlepped up the steps in this building that had no lift.

After an hour they arrived.

'What happened?' I said.

'The police have a terrorist alert and they are searching suspicious vans.'

I could picture the cops opening the doors of Rafi's van, with its tubes and pumps and all kinds of metal paraphernalia, methodically working their way through all these potential detonators, holding screwdrivers up to the light, 'Oy, this is going to take all morning . . .'

Rafi was handsome, dark; with him he had a tall blond kid who didn't talk. I think he was Romanian.

from another source, she submits that there might be a difference in usage between Jerusalem and Tel Aviv. Application was made by one riled emailer, in response to this, to the Institute of the Hebrew Language, the ultimate arbiter of all matters linguistic in Israel, instrumental as it is in bringing in words to form a modern tongue. However, it refused to do so on the grounds that sponjah is not a Hebrew word but a corruption of an English one and therefore beyond its remit. A further reader points out it is *nugnik*, not *nudnig*. The person in receipt of the magav from Roy, asks, 'Do you have a Hebrew language reader for the MS?' I have three.

'Rafi has a new Russki wife,' Yael said. 'Everyone is getting a Russki nowadays. Maybe I should find myself a Russki.'

Rafi did not speak English but he showed me the very nice chrome tap and shower attachment that was going to replace the plastic one and Yael told me how much I was going to have to pay for it.

They worked away in the bathroom.

My cellphone rang.

'Where are you?'

Where are you means where are you not. It means that there is a particular place where your friends and family don't want you to be, which has just been announced on the news. The caller was Ophir, one of the bedrocks of my time in Israel, who, eighteen months later, in July 2005, would be the first person to alert me to the terrorist attacks in London by ringing me and asking the exact same question – Where are you?

Ophir Wright, the protector, the enforcer. The person who takes a couple of hours off work to meet me at the airport, who tells me what's going on, who is in the news and who isn't, and what Lard Arse, the prime minister, has to say for himself, or . . . but Ophir's political opinions run to the slanderous, and are heavily spiked with offensive language and expletives. He is Israeli and British, but very much in that order, his Britishness a minor note, mainly manifested in a campaign to have the British Council hold a beer festival in Israel to promote English and Scottish ales.

'I'm at home,' I said.

'Turn on the tv. Sky are reporting it.'

'Yael,' I said, 'there's a *pigua*. I'm going to turn on the tv.'

Rafi and the Romanian boy heard the word *pigua* and they came in from the bathroom to watch the television.

The nice blonde English girl on Sky News was talking about a suicide bomb in the south of the city, on an intersection at

Allenby, the seedy, run-down end of this seedy, run-down city. An explosive flash appeared on the map. She had adopted the particular arrangement of features suitable for a Middle Eastern atrocity involving the killing of civilians. *Gravitas.* Which sat on her little face looking ill-adjusted, as if she had unexpectedly grown a big nose.

I told Yael what the newsreader was saying and she told Rafi and he told the Romanian, and in a variety of languages everyone got on the phone and rang their friends and said, 'Where are you?'

My phone rang once again. 'Where are you?' (my cousin), then again, 'Turn off Sky and watch Channel Two. I'll translate.'

'My landlady can translate, she's here, and a plumber, and a Romanian plumber's mate.'

'Why, you got a problem with the toilet?'

On Channel Two the blown-up façade of a currency exchange in one of the poorer parts of the city was on the screen. The fat religious men from Zaka were searching for body parts with special tweezers for eventual burial, because under the Jewish law the body must be interred entire. Three people had been murdered.

'This is worse than a *pigua*,' Yael said. And in disgust, Rafi and the Romanian trooped back into the bathroom and got on with the job of fixing the new taps to the wall, good and tight, so no stupid tourist would be able to pull them off.

The attack, we now learn, is a failed hit on Ze'ev Rosenstein, the Wolf, who is said to be one of the world's leading distributors of ecstasy pills, and has been spotted fleeing the scene, the announcer says. Like all outlaws he is fabled to be indestructible, or invincible, to have nine lives or be defended by special powers or devices, in his case a black armour-plated Mercedes protected by amulets attached to the dashboard, purchased by his devout wife from Sephardi rabbis in embroidered hats, who had personally blessed the amulets as a guarantee of defence against his enemies, the Abarjils of Lod and the Alperons of Givat Shmuel, who had already made numerous attempts to whack him.

'My grandfather called them *Yiddisher piraten*, Jewish pirates,' Ophir said.

Three innocent bystanders had been brutally killed in a failed mob hit. The *pigua*, the attacks by sweating, smiling Palestinian kids only a step away from heaven, were nothing you could do anything about. They were part of the great *balagan* that was Israeli life in those days of the second intifada, and the *shtarker* (the thug) in the Knesset, the prime minister, was doing what he could to protect them, or not, according to your political point of view.

Rafi and the Romanian screwed in the taps and tightened the bolts, I paid them five hundred shekels, and everyone left.

All day I was thinking about the bathroom, I couldn't get it out of my head. A nice placid tiled surface and behind it an unstoppable force which made me consider what other secrets the building harboured, apart from that cataract of water. Beyond the surface of the walls lurked all kinds of mysterious forces, electrical wires, rotting joists, timber eaten up by voracious termites. The façade of interior pleasantness was fraught with dangers I could do nothing to prevent.

And what had made Yael laugh, and what we were both laughing about, was the idea that you could control anything. For there is heaven and there is hell and in the middle there is the *balaganness* of life in all its absurdity. You try to tidy up the disorder, you do what you can to put things right, it's human nature.

So there I was, after everyone had left, sitting at my computer, a foreigner, writing everything down out of a writer's compulsion that there ought to be a record, an act of witness, in case everything went under, the really big *balagan* everyone was always worrying about in their neurotic, hysterical way, which being neurotic and hysterical myself, I fully understood, as a person saved from death by steak, and only twelve hours ago death by bathtub; that irresistible force that lies a few millimetres away, threatening to overwhelm us. And all you have to defend you is a set of cheap plastic taps and a plastic shower hose. What good will they do?

The shtarker, the mensch and the nebbish

When Ze'ev Rosenstein crashed through the tv screen into the Ruppin Street apartment on the day of the big *balagan*, I immediately recognised him as the descendant of all the Jewish tough guys who muscled in on our family dining table at home in Liverpool. Not in person, of course: my mother would never have let a gangster into the house, even if he was a bona fide citizen of the world's only Jewish state and in need of a table to put his feet under for Friday night dinner. But they were always around somewhere, leaning over my father's shoulder as he ate, stealing his homburg hats and lacing his conversation with their peppery phrases. 'What kind of racket is this?' my dad asked, as he examined the bill for my school fees.

In 1923, my father, a hungry, skinny nineteen-year-old, had jumped ship from his berth as a merchant seaman on the SS

Lacona, whose Ellis Island manifest lists him as 'Jew cook'. He spent the rest of the decade in New York, returning to Liverpool on the eve of the stock market crash, and until he died in 1983 he remained inside his imagination in the world he had had and then lost – that of the American gangsters he had watched eating cheesecake in Lindy's Delicatessen on Broadway, who occasionally patted him on the head and gave him an errand to run.

In the Damon Runyon stories he read and reread (and so did I), Lindy's was thinly disguised as Mindy's, but all the types were identifiable to him: Harry the Horse, Dave the Dude, the Lemon-drop Kid – little-league hoodlums he ran into while driving trucks of illegal beer over the Canadian border into upstate New York during Prohibition. Back home, walking on the shores of the Mersey in the 1930s, wearing a Panama beach suit and a straw hat, his Scouse accent sharpened by an American twang, he spoke of people like Dutch Schultz, Meyer Lansky and Louis Lepke, the then-rising stars of the Jewish underworld, but it was Arnold Rothstein who, for him, was the embodying myth of American immigration.

The gangster's biography sat in the bookcase next to the twin beds my parents slept in, removed a few spines along, for decency's sake, from the collected essays of Ralph Waldo Emerson and my mother's well-thumbed paperback editions of Harold Robbins. Rothstein, gunned down over a gambling debt in 1928, was a sophisticated fusion of brains, *chutzpah* and brutality, the man on whom F. Scott Fitzgerald would base the character of Meyer Wolfsheim in *The Great Gatsby*, the crook who was rumoured to have fixed the 1919 World Series. There had been New York Jewish gangsters before Rothstein: Monk Eastman, Kid Twist Zweibach, Big Jack Zelig, Dopey Benny Fein, Little Augie Fein and Kid Dropper, but they were just petty street thugs, immigrant kids trying to earn a bent living among the warring Irish and Italian gangs of old Manhattan.

Rothstein was the first person to see in Prohibition a business opportunity, a means to enormous wealth; he was the Moses of the Jewish gangsters, the progenitor, a rich man's son who showed the young hoodlums of the Bowery how to have style; indeed, the man who the Italian Lucky Luciano would later say taught him how to dress.

My father, the family man, the local businessman, the supporter of the synagogue, the protector of the virgin purity of his two daughters, loved Rothstein because of something that was embedded in the Jewish consciousness in those days, which reached its height in the 1930s when a Jew in Europe would turn on the radio and all he heard was bad news. The urgent need for a superhero, for a Jewish tough guy who could take on the bad men of Nazi Germany, was rooted inside my father and all of his generation who still had a small mental foothold in the inconsequential towns of eastern Europe.

For whatever else you might say about the gangsters, they never forget they were Jews. In 1945, Rueven Dafne, an emissary for the Haganah, met up with Bugsy Siegel in New York and asked him for money and guns. 'You mean to tell me Jews are fighting?' Siegel asked. 'You mean, fighting as in killing?' And hearing that it was true, Siegel replied, 'I'm with you,' and delivered a series of suitcases to Tel Aviv over the next few months filled with $5 and $10 bills amounting to $50,000.

The Soviet writer Isaac Babel summed up my father's feelings about gangsters in his story, 'How it was Done in Odessa', set among the hoodlums of that Black Sea port at the time of the Russian Revolution: 'Tartakovsky has the soul of a murderer, but he is one of us. He originated with us. He is our blood. He is our flesh, as though one momma had borne us.'

*

Ze'ev Rosenstein appeared on tv as a stocky, blockish, thick-necked figure with a bristly head, a schnitzel-and-chips kind of man, despite his million-and-a-half-dollar home in Hod HaSharon, a dormitory town near Tel Aviv. He was fifty and had grown up on the mean streets of Jaffa, where two families, Jewish and Arab mob bosses, had demonstrated that peace and co-existence were achievable by an equitable and just settlement, dividing between themselves the Tel Aviv drug trade.*

Mobsters like Rosenstein had been present in Palestine as far back as the 1930s, when eastern Europe emptied out its twilight population of gunmen and con artists. In 1972, Meyer Lansky, escaping the FBI at home, fled to Israel, seeking his right to become an Israeli citizen under the Law of Return, and was turned down by the prime minister herself, Golda Meir, the first Jew ever refused Aliyah. 'No gangsters in Israel,' she said. But the gangsters were there already.

Long before organised crime, the Jews had had their *shtarkers*: hard men, thugs. Back in the *shtetls* of eastern Europe, the

---

*Organised crime in Israel was set up along ethnic lines. Immigrants from the former Soviet Union specialised in sex slavery and prostitution; the Bedouin clans of the south smuggled women and drugs over the Egyptian border and dealt in stolen cars; Palestinian-Israelis distributed drugs; while the Jewish-Israeli crime families focused on *protekzia*, loan collection, and gambling. Rosenstein had already faced off the Aslans in the working-class Hatikvah neighbourhood of Tel Aviv in the late 1980s and early 1990s over gambling turf. His wealth grew from operating casinos in eastern Europe; at home a vacuum inside Israel was being filled with illegal gambling dens: seedy establishments advertising themselves as internet cafés or bingo parlours. At the beginning of 2000, Palestinian entrepreneurs in Jericho had built a fabulous new casino to which Israeli gamblers flocked. The West Bank town near the border with Jordan had the potential to become a new Las Vegas until the outbreak of the intifada later that year, which abruptly halted the flow of Israeli suckers across the Green Line.

villages and small towns where Jews lived a Yiddish life with all its economic and social aspects – its butcher, baker, rabbi, innkeeper, matchmaker, dressmaker, dairyman, miller, marriageable daughters, Talmudic scholars, revolutionaries hunched over tracts imported from Moscow and St Petersburg, Messianic Hassidim, small-time conmen and wealthy merchants – it was possible for everyone to exist within certain well-defined categories.

At the pinnacle of society was the *mensch*, a man, a human being in the fullest sense of what God had intended by the term, living a moral life based on hard work, charity and family values. To be a *mensch* was to be admired and respected, not merely for one's wealth or achievements (and a *mensch* always made sure his family was properly provided for), but for the essential decency and dignity of your being. A *mensch* always tried to do the right thing, to live his life humanely.

Various minor categories lay below: the *schlemiel*, the awkward individual who was always dropping his bowl of soup, and the *schlimazel*, the unfortunate on whom the soup got dropped.

There was an intellectual class, the *luftmensch*, who lived on air: he who starved his body to feed his mind, wandering from place to place in search of a crumb that would sustain his study.

And teeming those *shtetl* streets were the *nebbishes*, the early nerds: awkward and klutzy with their hands, neurotic, hypochondriacal, life's worriers for whom the Jewish telegram joke could have been invented – Start worrying. Details to follow.

Famous examples of the *mensch* exist in literature and film. Primo Levi was a *mensch*, the survivor whose great literary powers allowed him to explore the inner world of death camps, to interrogate their terrible moral meanings. Woody Allen is a *nebbish*, the harmless, puny, witty Jew who fights back armed with nothing more than *chutzpah*. Though before Levi became a *mensch*, he was a *nebbish*.

On the outskirts of the *shtetl*, along the rutted muddy road that led out of town to the dangerous lands, another type was lurking, about whom no one ever said much. Every so often a kid was born with a build like an ox; too stupid to advance in school or make much of himself in business, he would be posted like a hulking, animated scarecrow outside the village.

The *shtarker*, the Jewish thug, was there to scare off your enemies. He was not someone you boasted about, but nonetheless it was possible to have a sneaking admiration for a Jew who could see off the marauding Cossacks with his fists instead of weasely appeals to their better nature or those scheming attempts to outmanoeuvre them, which became the subject of so many Jewish jokes.

Ze'ev Rosenstein was a *shtarker*, as were all his enemies, the rival gangs that tried to whack him. The prime minister of Israel was also a *shtarker*, a thug in a military uniform who baffled the liberal West which wanted to think well of the Jews, those incubators of world culture who had produced Primo Levi, Spinoza, Kafka, Mahler, Proust, Joseph Roth – *nebbishes*, all.

The Israelis liked Ariel Sharon in the same way and for exactly the same reasons that my father had liked Arnold Rothstein, and why Israelis were secretly excited by Ze'ev Rosenstein.

Sharon attracted shame and admiration. His obesity, his shady past, his bullying, his indifference to murder, his corruption, his *lobbishe* sons, the rumours about his marriages, everything about him made you cringe when you saw him on tv, particularly on the BBC. The Jews wanted a *shayner Yid*, a beautiful Jew, like Yitzhak Rabin, to be their representative, but they kept on winding up with these loud-mouthed former terrorists and war criminals. I was always being asked, plaintively, why the Jews chose brutes to represent them. Surely the Knesset had more to offer than this, such as the modestly spoken former mayor of

Haifa, Amram Mitzna, who had so disastrously lost to Sharon
when he ran for office for the second time. But Mitzna was a
yekke, a German Jew, a type of whom it was said in Palestine in
the 1930s that instead of a heart they had a clock. They were
above all the Yiddish categories because they were not Yiddim –
Jews, but not Jew-ish. Respected, usually on the extreme left, but
rarely loved, they were intellectuals who could win the Nobel
Prize for this or that, but in their company you couldn't sit
around with your feet up on the coffee table, telling jokes,
waving your arms around and talking with your mouth full.

The *shtarker* does not bring you *yiches*, that sense of pride and
honour that is bestowed on the family and indeed the whole
community when, say, a Jew or an Israeli wins the Nobel. The
shtarker is a necessary fact of this terrible life. We have one in
the Bible.

Unlike the prophets, Samson doesn't get a book of his own. He
puts in his first appearance in Judges chapter 13, during the
period when the Jews are under occupation by the Philistines.
Samson is the product of divine infertility treatment. His father,
Menorah, and wife (unnamed) do a deal with God, who promises a son to deliver the Jews from colonialism as long as Samson
never cuts his hair. Samson's progress through the verses is a list
of murder and massacre, revenge and counter-revenge. For relax-
ation he sleeps with *shiksa* prostitutes in Gaza. Every time
Samson brandishes his ass's jawbone and murders a few more
Philistines, God couldn't be more delighted. Samson, like the
Golem (the medieval Prague progenitor of Frankenstein's monster, built by a rabbi to fight anti-Semitism), has been specifically
created to be the defender of the Jews. After Delilah, in the pay
of the Philistines, persuades him to reveal the secret of his
strength, and cuts his hair while he is sleeping, his eyes are put
out and the enemies of the Jews 'offer a great sacrifice unto

Dagon their god . . . for they say, Our god hath delivered into our hands our enemy, and the destroyer of our country, which slew many of us.'

But the cretinous Philistines don't realise that while Samson languishes in prison his hair is growing. They take him out for a bit of sport and tie him to the pillars of the building. Samson prays to God to grant him the strength to deliver a final crushing revenge. Straining his muscles, he brings down the prison on top of him, with three thousand people gathered on the roof, 'so the dead which he slew at his death were more than they which he slew in his life'. The first suicide bomber!

When Philip Roth interviewed Primo Levi in 1986, he criticised *If Not Now, When?* (Levi's novel about Jewish partisans during the war), which he described as 'more narrowly tendentious . . . than the impulse that generates the autobiographical works'. Levi replied, a little defensively: 'I wished to assault a commonplace still prevailing in Italy: a Jew is a mild person, a scholar (religious or profane), unwarlike, humiliated, who tolerated centuries of persecution without ever fighting back. It seemed to me a duty to pay homage to those Jews who, in desperate conditions, found the courage and skill to resist.'

Even Levi fancied himself as something of a *shtarker*. Indeed, his capture by the Germans was due to an ill-fated flirtation with the partisan life.

Thus the *mensch*, the *nebbish* and the *shtarker* are the three figures which form the true trinity of Jewish culture, and they come together in the stories of Isaac Babel – of the Jewish gangsters of Odessa and of a Jew incongruously serving in a Cossack regiment during the civil war. Babel based his stories on his own self, a child of stunted growth growing up to be a writer, 'with spectacles on his nose and autumn in his heart'. His father's escape fantasy for Isaac, the son born in Odessa in 1894 during the period of state-sponsored pogroms against the Jews, was that he might become an infant prodigy on the violin, performing before the crowned heads of Europe. Like the immigrant Jews of New York, Babel was drawn, instead, to the Jewish gangsters of his city. As a young intellectual during the Revolution, he took the advice of Maxim Gorky and went 'among the people'.

When the American critic Lionel Trilling wrote an introduction to the (incomplete) 1955 Penguin edition of the stories, he saw as the principal joke of the 'Red Cavalry' stories the anomaly of having, as their main character, a Jew who is a member of a Cossack regiment, traditionally the persecutors of the Jews. The Cossack, he wrote, 'stood in total antithesis to the principle of the Jew's existence. The Jew conceived his own ideal character to consist in his being intellectual, pacific, humane. The Cossack was physical, violent, without mind or manners . . . the enemy not only of the Jew . . . but the enemy also of all men who thought of liberty; he was the natural and appropriate instrument of ruthless oppression.'

But to nineteenth-century Russian intellectuals, including Tolstoy, Trilling points out, the Cossack was rather an appealing figure: 'He was the man as yet untrammelled by civilisation, direct, immediate, fierce. He was the man of enviable simplicity, the man of the body – and of the horse, the man who moved with speed and grace . . . For [Tolstoy] the Cossack was indeed the noble savage, all too savage, not often noble, yet having in his savagery some quality that might raise strange questions in a Jewish mind.'

Thus Trilling saw in the figure of the Cossack a yearning in Babel to throw off his own liberal, intellectual instincts, an itch in him to become part of a people of the body rather than a people of the head. He points to the story which exposes the psychic divisions within Babel's mind during this period. In 'After the Battle', the narrator is discovered to have gone into battle with no ammunition in his gun; he is accused of being a member of the Molokan Sect – a pacifist and God-worshipper. But this is not it at all. Trudging through the rain, the narrator pleads for a favour, 'imploring fate to grant me the simplest of proficiencies – the ability to kill my fellow-man'. This sentiment in Babel's mouth is, Trilling says, only partly ironic.

The period between the 1880s and the start of the First World War offered Jews in eastern Europe three possible means of re-invention: the first was emigration to America, where the Jewish gangsters of Odessa would thrive in the fresh air of American capitalism; the second was Zionism, which was in the process of discarding the neurasthenic *shtetl* Jew and re-engineering his soul in preparation for the outdoor life of the kibbutz; the third was the Russian Revolution, in which Jews were to play a leading role.

Those who adopted this final option abandoned the mystical baggage of an ancient religion and their predicament as a tiny persecuted minority, protected only by their irksome status as God's chosen people; they abandoned their history for the Marxist notion of History. They signed up for equality, freedom and rights accorded to them by virtue of their class. October 1917 was the defining moment when the *mensch* and the *shtarker* were joined together. It was a Jewish dream come true. Only through violence could man liberate himself from oppressive forces, but violence in their hands was not mindless. It served a revolutionary ideology, which would bring justice to suffering mankind.

Of those three choices Jews of the time could make, this turned out to be the very worst. Babel was murdered by firing squad in Moscow's Lubyanka prison in 1940 at the age of forty-five, on a trumped-up espionage confession after unsuccessfully begging to be allowed to finish his only novel. Of those Russian Jews who emerged blinking into the tail end of the century in 1992 and emigrated to Israel, some were scientists, some were

chess grand masters, some were prima ballerinas; others formed
the country's new industry of organised crime, drug dealing and
prostitution – the *shtarker* with all the *mensch*-like elements corroded by seventy-five years of Soviet socialism. According to
eyewitness Palestinian accounts of the Israeli incursions into
Jenin, many of the soldiers were recent immigrants from Russia
who spoke little Hebrew and who looted the homes of civilians.
Their hatred of Muslims did not suddenly appear out of nowhere,
inculcated by the Israeli state, but was nurtured during the
exceptionally brutal wars in Afghanistan and Chechnya.

Ze'ev Rosenstein and Ariel Sharon, each in their way, answered
a need in Israeli society that went deeper than politics, occupation, intifada, failed peace agreements or the founding of the
state.

In order for an Israeli to write poetry, or make millions on the
stock market, or act in a movie and win an Oscar, in order to be
ordinarily useful and productive, he required a kind of mental
protection, the idea that the *shtarker* was outside the village with
his ass's club. In the 1950s the Jewish gangsters of America began
to die out as a force in organised crime; unlike the Italians, they
did not found families; they did not send their sons to the streets,
they sent them to law school. People felt that now Jews were
entering the full life of America, the suburban dream, there was
no more need for them to turn to violence, but perhaps the truth
was that the Jews no longer needed their *shtarkers* at home – they
had the Israeli army, Jewish soldiers with a gun, the Uzi, actually
designed and invented by a Jew.

Rosenstein did nothing for the good of the state, but he and
Sharon were from the same mould and impulse. Like Babel's
gangsters in pre-Revolutionary Odessa, in particular Benya
Krik – with his 'lightning-quick beginning and his terrible end'
who 'talks little, but he talks with zest. He talks little, but you

want he'll say more' – they were men. The Benya Kriks drove around in loud motor cars and wore raspberry-coloured boots and chocolate jackets, watch straps with diamond bracelets. They did not keep their head down and avoid trouble. A community bound by laws designed to contain and persecute them saw and marvelled at outrageous characters who defied all laws, whether they came from the court system or the United Nations.

The Jewish revolutionaries promised universal equality; the Jewish gangsters, anarchic and individualistic, and the Jewish thug who ran Israel offered something else: 'And he got his way, that Benya Krik, because he was passionate, and passion holds sway over the universe.'

Batei Café

When I think back to my time in Tel Aviv I think of an end-less tour of cafés, and the people I met in them. In Israel I had an intellectual life I have never experienced anywhere else in the world. The café society of the city was not Israel, it did not represent the views of the majority, far from it, but Israelis did not really understand that there are few cities in the Western world any more where a man or a woman can walk a few metres to their *beit café* (coffee shop, plural *batei*), order a cap-puccino or latte, sit down with their newspaper and in a few minutes be talking about epistemology, false consciousness, Iranian theocracy, the Swedish novel and neo-colonialism. Not all of these conversations took place with people on the left; there were plenty of people who would tell you why it was a good idea to build a fence across the West Bank and asked why the BBC and CNN seemed to hate Jews, but even so, you could not help but think that it was oxygen to the brain to be discussing Kant instead of (in an ironic, postmodern, culturally critical way, of course) Kylie Minogue's breast cancer, or *Celebrity Big Brother.*

A few times a week, around 11am, I would walk to a café called Patisserie, near Rabin Square where a religious hothead had assassinated the prime minister in 1995 while he was addressing a peace rally. The owner, Gary, made marvellous breads and jams and had a sideline catering parties for the British Council. Sitting at her usual table, reading the newspapers, my friend Michal would point out to me the day's top stories and translate them into English, and after half an hour or so she would get on the phone to her husband, Irish Thomas, and tell him, 'Bounder, get out of bed and come to the coffee shop.' I can't remember why she started calling him Bounder, an English term to describe a cad, but they had a running joke that he was always going to disappear one day, and if he went out to do the grocery shopping and took longer than expected, she would tell me, 'You see? It's what we always thought, he's MI5, or is it MI6? I can never remember which one is the British spy service.'

Michal had two switches: first, the evil conniving corrupt lying politicians that ran the country, and the idiots who elected them, 'like retarded children that the rest of class has to wait to catch up until they finally understand that you cannot occupy another people forever and so brutally'; and second, shopping. 'You see this necklace? It's from a new store I found, you want to go there? I have a hair appointment at 11.30, just a blow job, but we could go after that, the prices are great.'

She was bitter about Israel. Her parents were South African Jews who in 1948, the year the Nationalists were elected and enacted the apartheid laws, out of disgust and idealism had sold their vineyards in Stellenbosch on the Cape and moved to a kibbutz in the newly established state of Israel . . . 'and how do you think they feel *now*?'

On the kibbutz in the 1950s she had grown up in a socialist system so exacting that its strict rules against private property extended even to clothing; all her shopping impulses grew out of that blouse with the puffed sleeves which an aunt had sent her from South Africa, and according to the kibbutz regulations had to be shared by all the other girls of her age, who would take it in turns to wear it, and it would come to her last, when it was torn and stained. Because it was important even for little girls to learn that capitalism's fetishisation of consumer goods had no place in the idealised socialist experiment where urban Jews were being retrained as peasants.*

In the army, during the period known as the War of Attrition, between the end of the Six Day War and the start of the Yom Kippur War, she served in intelligence, crouching in a fox hole monitoring the radio messages of the UN, the *umnikim* as the Israelis called them, while her Russian-born friend monitored the radio messages of Soviet 'advisers' who were training the Egyptians to use SAM 6 and 7 anti-aircraft missiles. In lulls in the fighting, they tried to straighten their curly hair by winding it into giant rollers, and had difficulty fitting their headphones over them.

---

*Michal wrote, after reading this: 'I know it's bon ton to slander kibbutz life and blame everything on growing up there, probably as part of worshipping American politics and Thatcherism, and besmirching anything even slightly socialist. But actually I have very fond memories of the kibbutz, maybe because my parents were among the founding members and living on the kibbutz, while other kids were orphans or were sent there because their parents couldn't look after them.'

She met her husband Thomas, a Tipperary Irish Catholic Israeli citizen, when he was the foreign editor of the *Jerusalem Post* where they both then worked.

What did her family think of her marrying a non-Jew?

'Listen, by the time I married Thomas, I was already in my forties, and they were desperate. Thomas made jokes about jumping out the balcony and said he was surprised my brothers-in-law didn't come with us to lie guard on the stairway with shotguns outside our room all night – just to make sure he didn't sneak away.'

The years of the intifada and the Oslo years before them had turned Michal and Thomas into bitter cynics. The solution seemed to them so obvious – end the occupation, withdraw to the 1967 borders, divide Jerusalem and come to a realistic agreement about the fate of the Palestinian refugees – and they were enraged that neither their government, nor the general population that had voted for it, could see what was staring them in the face. Michal had been on the platform at the peace rally the night that Rabin was assassinated; she smelt the mood of the country after it, she knew what was coming. She predicted that his successor, Shimon Peres, would not win the next election; she felt viscerally the lurch to the right which she was powerless to prevent. Her own newspaper, the *Jerusalem Post*, had been bought by Conrad Black, the right-wing Canadian proprietor of the *Daily Telegraph* in London. All the left-wing staff were laid off, one by one, and she, the union representative, was left to negotiate their redundancy pay. She had been the paper's political correspondent who knew everyone and Thomas would pick up the phone some mornings to find a government minister barking at him: 'Tell your wife I don't like what she wrote about me in the newspaper today.' They had moved her sideways to consumer editor before firing her, and now she worked as a translator on the English-language edition of *Ha'aretz*, the country's left-of-centre paper.

'This disengagement plan,' Thomas said, talking of the newly hatched proposal to pull the settlers unilaterally out of Gaza, 'it's just a ruse by Sharon to divert attention away from the Greek island affair. It will be quietly dropped within a month, wait and see.' The prime minister was under investigation for financial corruption, involving one of his sons and some holiday developments in Greece. It seemed inevitable to us that he would be driven from office.

'It will never happen, this so-called disengagement,' said Michal. 'We know these people, you think they'll go against the settlers? Forget it.'

So we yakked and yakked, reading the tea leaves, predicting the future, which was all you could do, apart from sign petitions against the occupation, and feel powerless.

In another café, closer to home, one building down on Mapu Street up a flight of steps, I would go in the evening for a glass of wine, or in the afternoon for coffee when I came to check my email at the internet place next door. I felt at home there, not just because of the warm welcome from the owner, Moishe, who looked like Elvis Presley in his early prime, and Efrat, the Yemenite waitress (who resembled the drawings in my Collins Junior Bible of the beautiful Hebrew maiden walking to the well with a clay pot balanced gracefully on her head), and her neurotic, screwed-up boyfriend Andrew, from Seattle, whose story took him two hours to tell one evening, and I'd tell it here but he wants to be a writer and so deserves the chance to tell it himself.

Café Mapu, because of its intimate size and location in the centre of the Bauhaus city, was a place that had always attracted writers, editors, academics, even before Moishe bought it, and it was really easy to fall into conversation. Sometimes a transvestite would be sitting sipping coffee at the bar discussing with Moishe the role of Yasser Arafat as symbol. The French woman who did shifts at the internet shop next door would be there, and her co-worker, the son of Filipino diplomats, who collected photographs of soldiers on his digital camera.

I used to run into Fabiana, the Argentinian-born fiction editor who came to Israel in 1973 when she was thirteen, at the time of the Dirty War at home, the time of the Generals and the Disappeared, and we would talk about Borges, the Talmud, psychoanalysis and other matters considered vital to the life of Tel Aviv café culture, which began in the 1930s with the building of the White City, created out of concrete, drawing the heat through its thin walls and driving the inhabitants out onto the streets in the evening in search of cool sea breezes. And having fled there from Berlin and Vienna, what could be a more natural way to spend a few hours than sitting over coffee and cake, discussing ideas, just as they had done at home, in Europe?

'I envy you,' Fabiana said.

'For what?'

'Living in London, where every night you can go to the Groucho Club and listen to all the leading minds talking about literature and philosophy.'

When she had wiped off the coffee that forced itself, like a high-velocity hose, from my mouth onto her chest, she listened while I explained that the only discussions that took place in London clubs concerned money, deals, contracts, sex and cocaine. And that no, Martin Amis and Ian McEwan did not sit at a table every night in Soho, talking about Dostoevsky.

Then she would begin to discuss the Palestinians, particularly the suicide bombers and their mothers who expressed their deep pleasure at their sons' deeds and wished for more sons to offer themselves as *shahids*.

'Barbarians,' she said.

*

A block away, on Gordon Street, the street of the art galleries, was Café Tam. A small garden set back from the traffic shaded the rickety tables and bougainvillea sent shocks of flowers over the awning.

It was another place that did an excellent breakfast, omelette with a selection of cheeses, tomato and cucumber salad, a basket of breads and preserves. Gadi Taub, the former children's television presenter who had lived in London in his childhood and was enraptured by the television programme *Jackanory*, would be working at his laptop on his doctorate, a critique of the philosopher Richard Rorty.

Behind me, two men were speaking in English, talking about Salman Rushdie. The older man, with a small pointed grey beard, was trying to glimpse the cover of my book, which was Fouad Ajami's *Dream Palace of the Arabs*. When I got up to leave, he stopped me.

'What are you reading?'

I showed him.

'What's it about?'

'Arab culture.'

'What Arab culture? The Arabs have no culture.'

'Why are you speaking to each other in English?'

'I don't have good Hebrew.'

'How long have you been here?'

'That's a good question, sit down, join us. I first came here in the 1950s but in the 1970s I went to Greece. I've been living in Athens until a couple of years ago.'

'Where were you born?'

'Hungary.'

'How did you survive the Holocaust?'

'I was saved by Raoul Wallenberg.'

'Really?' said the other man. 'I never knew that.'

'And you?' I asked him.

'I am not a Jew, but I am the father of Jews. I come from Brazil; I was making my way overland to India in the early 1970s and I met a girl here and never left.'

'Why?'

'One thing you can say about this place, at least it's not boring.'

'How do you two know each other?'

'We go way back, we used to live on an international anarchist commune in the Sinai desert.'

'That's right,' the Brazilian-Israeli told me, 'and we've never forgiven Menahem Begin for handing it back to the Egyptians.'

Chaverim

Jerusalem sat, sits, on me like a lead helmet. Nothing about it excited or interested me, including the wretched freezing winters, the awful restaurants, the feeling I had that if I didn't watch my step I'd fall down a hole any minute into the fourth century BC, and however much I shouted no one would come and rescue me from that horrible crevasse. I distrusted the atmosphere at the American Colony hotel in East Jerusalem, the Arab city. The minute you put a foot across the door from the car park with all the UN vehicles and the cars with the diplomatic plates or 'TV' taped across the roof, you stepped out of the country into a sumptuous interior, tinkling fountains, lovely tiles, perfect gracious service from the Palestinian waiters who made a safe space here for the foreigners, an international no-man's land where old friends greeted each other, 'Hey! Haven't seen you since

Baghdad.' 'Didn't we meet during Kosovo?' 'Yeah, I think I still have your card.' 'Let's go to the bar.'

From the American Colony you were serviced by Palestinian organisations which assisted you in entering the occupied territories of the West Bank and Gaza, providing you with cars with Palestinian plates and the word 'Press' in Arabic, Hebrew and English stencilled on the side; with fixers, translators, press officers – everything you needed to form a swift impression of the essential facts on the ground of the occupation.

Here is a soldier whose face is hidden behind a helmet, who might actually be made of metal and webbing, who does not come from a place but is prefabricated in a factory somewhere at the back of the ministry of defence. And here is a refugee who works in a garage in Ramallah, whose boss shouts at him all day long, and when a microphone is thrust at him by the world-famous CNN, he gulps and says the words you have to say when someone turns a tv camera on you, the ones the politicians always speak, so they must be right, that we will never rest until we reclaim our land that was stolen from . . . and the viewers back home in America turn to each other and, according to their point of view, they say, 'See?'

Sometimes the journalists ventured into West Jerusalem where an ageing population of religious Jews in beards and hats and long dresses and wigs formed a backdrop of exotic extras. And in the old city itself, the Armenians, the Greek Orthodox, the Lubavitch, the guardians of the Al-Aqsa mosque, everyone was planting a stake in this weird piece of contested ground. Everyone was in costume, dressed as symbols, so you could tell straight away what you are supposed to know about how they thought and felt.

I saw a pair of twins once, American giants in their sixties, each with a spade-shaped grey beard and a blanket tied with rope over their Levis and Timberland boots, telling a Hassid (an ultra-Orthodox Jew) that back home in Texas they had received a message from the Lord telling them to make their way to the Holy Land to convert the Jews to Christianity. The Hassid smiled into his beard. Who needed the cinema or tv with their naked women and other immodest sights, when you could have all the entertainment you needed right here on the street?

I saw, by the Wailing Wall, a young soldier at the kiosk at the side of the men's section being kitted out to pray with *tallis*, *kippah*, *tephilin* wound around his forearm, and he began to sway back and forth under its old stones until, after a minute or so, his cellphone rang, and he tore off all this religious paraphernalia. Maybe he was called away by his commanding officer, or by his friends to come and meet them for coffee, or by his mother screaming at him for something he did or, more likely, forgot to do.

In the Old City another time, I noticed that my watch had stopped around twenty minutes earlier, just as I entered at the Jaffa Gate. Later in the morning, I took it into a jeweller's to have the battery replaced, and he picked it up and showed me the second hand turning. There's nothing wrong with this, he told me, and looking at the time on its face, I noticed that it had started again the minute I left those high, harsh, seductive walls, away from all that *meshuggenah* intensity that gave me a bad headache.

God forbid a journalist should venture onto the coastal plain that stretches from Haifa in the north to Ashkelon in the south, where Israelis live when they have taken off their metal exteriors and hung them in the cupboard and revealed themselves to be just men, after all, not robots. For as the novelist Aharon Appelfeld had told me, 'to the rest of the world an Israeli is a man who wakes up in the morning, has breakfast, gets into his tank which is parked outside his apartment, and drives to Nablus.'

It was on the coastal plain that I spent most of my time, well away from Jerusalem, only going in when I wanted to meet up with Aharon and David Grossman, whose attachment to that city is part of them, not me. I would sit in the living room of my *chaverim*, friends, Yan and Rosita, turning the pages of their family album. Their house in the suburbs of Rehovot had been designed specially for them by an architect; Rosita had taken charge. She made him give her a large, beautiful kitchen where she prepared huge meals, mainly meat, because Yan was a carnivore and he distrusted vegetables and slow cooking. For him, the important room was his library which housed all the books that piqued his imagination, from José Saramago to Terry Pratchett. He devoured literature in English and Russian. And in the afternoons and early evenings they sat in their garden shaded by palm trees, a family of young owls nesting in them – a picture he captured with his expensive camera and emailed to me. He had photographs of ibex in the desert. They had settled inside that house with its comforts and pleasures. Still, there was a certain restless element left inside Yan, and in a small room which housed his computer he sat reading pages off the internet, from the international press, and sent me links and said, 'Who is this person, writing this?' He is funny, acid, sarcastic and clever. I sent him a link to a blog written by a Marxist who nonetheless supported the Iraq war. 'See, when I look at this Marxist,' he responded, 'I remember that I still need to carry a sharp knife.'

I have never met a family whose personal story, its tragedy and comedy, is so entwined with the history of a century. A hundred years ago, when my parents' parents left Poland and Russia, running away, as they thought, from Europe, Yan and Rosita's parents stayed. They were from Moldova, which at the time of their birth was in Romania. Ethnic Moldovans were considered second-class citizens in Romania, Yan told me: 'The Moldovans were barely above Gypsies. Still considered the same, although god knows what these Romanians have to brag about. The Russian-speaking part of the population, which included most Jewish families, was relatively privileged, even up to separate Russian schools. The part where my parents were born became Soviet in 1940, a bit before the war – see, for me World War Two still counts from 1941, the German invasion of the USSR. Old habits die hard.'

Yan himself was born in Kishinev, a famous town in Jewish memory for its horrific pogrom. At Easter 1903 a youth named Michael Rybalenko was found dead in the town of Dabossary, and, although it was later proved that he was killed by his uncle, a rumour spread that he had been murdered by Jews to obtain blood for the making of the Passover matzo – that old medieval blood libel which began in thirteenth-century Norwich (and became the basis for Chaucer's 'The Prioress's Tale') and hence the opportunity for the expulsion of the Jews from England. The Moldovan blood libel was fanned by the local, government-subsidised newspaper, Bessarabetz, which called for the death of Russian Jews in revenge. A second rumour spread, that the Jews had killed a Christian servant girl, and on Easter Sunday a mob began to attack Jewish homes and shops in Kishinev; rioting lasted for three days until, not before time, Russian troops intervened, but by then forty-seven Jews had been killed and over five hundred wounded.

This pogrom had been the final straw for my grandparents; because of Kishinev, they left eastern Europe and never, for a moment, thought of returning, never set foot again, not even once, on the soil of eastern Europe, until I did, in the mid-1990s, and visited Lomza, the town of my father's birth: 70 per cent Jewish in 1905, 50 per cent Jewish in 1939 and no Jews at all after 1943, when those who had remained were rounded up and taken to the forest and shot, according to a plaque on a wall of what had once been a Jewish house. The derelict Jewish cemetery was full of gravestones, sticking up out of the trim grass like broken teeth, defaced with swastikas and slogans, '*Jude Raus*' (Jews out, though they were all out already) and, in English, 'White Power'.

The pogrom at Kishinev was the source, too, of another beginning and ending. Haim Bialik, the first Hebrew poet of the modern era, who took up Ben Yehuda's challenge and began to write modern poetry in what had been a dead tongue, was so moved and enraged by what had happened at Kishinev that he wrote his most famous poem, 'City of the Killings', with the following lines carefully read and discussed by the early Zionists for their portentous content.

And now go and I'll bring you to the places where they
    hid
the out house, the pigpen and the other places smeared
    with shit
and you'll see with your own eyes where they were
    concealed – your brothers, your people
the descendants of the Maccabees, the great
    grandchildren of lions
from 'Merciful Father' and the seed of the great 'martyrs'
were twenty souls in one hole and thirty upon thirty
and they have made great my place in the world and
    sanctified my name to the multitudes . . .
They fled the flight of mice and hid like tics
and died like dogs there where they were found
and tomorrow morning – when the fugitive son comes out
and finds the corpse of his father – smeared and
    despised –

and why do you weep, son of man, and why do you hide
your face in your hand? Gnash your teeth and dissolve.*

Contemporary Israeli writers are always being asked if literature
can change the world. Bialik's poem was a message to the Jews.
Why didn't you fight back? Why are you so spineless and cow-
ardly? Why don't you take your fate into your own hands? Don't
you remember your forefathers, the Maccabees? Thus Zionism
was ignited, by poetry, and Bialik became Israel's national poet.
Later, in the 1950s, someone would ask the fatal question of the
Holocaust, 'Why did the Jews go like sheep to the slaughter?'
And many Jews took that question personally, as they had done
Bialik's stinging words, and decided that the Jews' best defence
was going to be not only retaliating, but getting the retaliation in
first, to be on the safe side and to make sure the enemy knew
what was what.

So if my grandparents, across the border in Poland and the
Ukraine, saw what was up after Kishinev, why didn't the grandparents of Yan and Rosita? Yan found it difficult to answer this
question, people see things in different ways. Some had left; one
great-uncle went to America and became a millionaire, another
in the 1920s went to Palestine and started a construction company and was still there when the rest of the family arrived in
1980, still drinking vodka in the hot sun of the Middle East. But
of the family that stayed, there were revolutionary firebrands,
fighters in the Spanish Civil War, heroes of the Red Army, and
an unfortunate brother who tried to swim across the river Dniestr
from Romania into the Soviet Union. 'He was trying to reach
the socialist heaven and got sixteen years in Gulag instead,' Yan
said. 'The supremely cruel thing was that his other brother was

*'City of the Killings' from *Songs of Bialik*, translated by Atar Hadari,
Syracuse University Press, 2000

not told anything about the fate of the second one. Luckily, Rosita's father escaped the Gulag; the NKVD was not very thorough after all.'

In the pages of the album, the hero of the Red Army and the Spanish anti-fascist campaign appears on his own page in a studio portrait. His Jewish face looks out beneath a carapace of medals and red stars, eerily resembling my own uncles, those soft-handed businessmen and ebullient wives with Madeira lace tablecloths in suburban semi-detached houses, having afternoon tea in the garden on cool summer days, my cousins and I fighting under the table among our parents' legs. He could have been seated at our family gatherings, that Moishe or Abie, whatever his name was, but instead he was up to his neck in snow and Nazi bullets and stirring songs about the proletariat.

Yan and Rosita had been born during the period of the Doctor's Plot, in Stalin's final, demented years when he became convinced that a cabal of Jewish doctors was trying to murder him, igniting a wave of state-sponsored anti-Semitism in the USSR. And both their parents were doctors. Another effect of the time in which Yan was born was that his father, even though he was a gynaecologist who delivered the babies of all the local party officials, did not dare circumcise his own son.

Yan's mother and father lived less than a hundred metres away from their own parents, and as a child he passed back and forth between these two worlds: the Soviet Union of Khrushchev, the space race with the Americans, the revelations at the XXIInd Party Congress of the extent of the savage butchery of the Stalin years – and his grandparents' household, Yiddish-speaking Zionists, who listened carefully on the radio for other news.

He was an adored child, an only son, who got everything he wanted. Until he was sixteen he was a gung-ho enthusiastic communist – an adolescent disorder, he would later think.

Clever Jews in the Soviet Union in the 1960s did not become lawyers or doctors or study for MBAs, they were destined to be scientists. The leading scientific institution in the USSR was the University of Moscow, but like American universities in the 1930s it had strict quotas for the number of Jews it would accept. Both Yan and Rosita went to the University of Novosibirsk, in Siberia, the intellectual powerhouse of the country – which at its height had 70 per cent Jewish students. Yan enrolled in the physics programme, Rosita in chemistry.

The photographs of them from that time are, to me, immensely touching. We are all the same age, born in 1951. At twenty-two Yan and Rosita are already married. Yan has observed Rosita hesitate for half an hour at an airport stand selling fresh juices, unable to decide which of the two available to choose, and at that moment knows that this will be his wife because she will always require his guidance. (He tells this story ironically, as a man who has, some time later, discovered a political discourse called male chauvinism.) There is already a baby which he does not see until she is two months old because of a combination of end-of-semester exams and the lack of the necessary funds to travel from Novosibirsk back to Moldova where Rosita is with her family, giving birth.

In the photographs, Rosita is wearing lisle stockings that hang in wrinkles round her knees and ankles. 'It was very difficult to find fashionable clothes at that period,' she tells me. She is a slender, almost ethereal girl, with wavy brown hair and soft brown eyes, and Yan, dark, handsome, ardent, eager, looks at her as though he has won the Lenin Prize.

They left the Soviet Union both because they were sickened by the system and because of anti-Semitism. 'There was anti-Semitism on two levels,' Yan's brother-in-law Yuri told me one afternoon, when Yan gathered together the old gang from Novosibirsk in the living room of the house in Rehovot. 'There was everyday anti-Semitism where you would be told that your nationality was Jewish – it was Lenin who first came up with this idea, by the way – and you should go to Israel, though of course they wouldn't let you. Then there was official anti-Semitism, which you felt every time you tried to get a job. I was told to my face that I wouldn't be hired because I was Jewish, and you couldn't get a place at the best universities.'

Yuri had been a close friend of the son of Donald Maclean, one of the Cambridge spies who fled to the Soviet Union in 1953 after they were uncovered as moles inside British intelligence. 'When they arrived, they were told to pick a different surname,' Yuri said, 'and they chose Ferguson, but the KGB said it wasn't a good name.' It sounded, to the Russians, too much like the Yiddish *fergessen* – to forget. 'They stuck with it, though, and when he applied to university he had to get a letter from the KGB certifying that he wasn't a Jew.'

Many of the Russian Jews, reacting both to anti-Semitism as well as the Soviet system, moved far to the right when they left the country. A million Russian Jews (including around two hundred thousand who were not Jews, but wives and husbands, or those whose Jewish origins were so watered down that they were now practising Christians) had arrived in Israel since 1992 and formed one of the most right-wing voting blocs in the country. The 'Russians' (Yan would always put inverted commas round the word to make a distinction between the Russian Jews and the ones who considered themselves to be ethnic Russians) gathered in the living room that afternoon were not right-wingers, but they were still angry with the European left for 'believing the propaganda about the Soviet Union when the facts were there for all to see,' said Gregory, a mathematician who came to Israel in 1996. It was useless to explain to him that the European left had many faces and many ideologies. The left's defence of Marxism, together with its anti-Zionism, was like a vice, a mechanism which crushed these Russian Jews and left them with no physical or political place.

'Even though I belong to the left, I understand the right,' said Mark. 'For decades we were second-class citizens in the Soviet Union. Different people came here for different reasons but they all wanted to think of themselves as strong, and proud. When the Russian teenagers died in the Dolphinarium terrorist attack, the country said, "Now you are the same as us." What to do about terrorism? In Russia, it had always been acceptable to use force to come to solutions. If you are in power, you use force to show that you are right.'

Yan and Rosita left Russia and emigrated to Israel in 1980, together with their two children and Yan's parents. They decided to immerse themselves in the new country, to be Israelis from the word go. Their close friend Yossi, from the university, arrived in the country via another path. In 1984, while on holiday in the Crimea, he met Galina, a non-Jewish woman who had been born in Weimar, East Germany, where her father was part of the occupying Soviet forces. When she was three, the family returned home, to Lvov in the Ukraine, and later to Novosibirsk, where she grew up. She was politically active in the party, a member of the Young Pioneers communist youth movement for the training of future leaders. She became a teacher and got married and together with her husband they had a son. The meeting in the Crimea broke up two marriages and later produced, for Galina and Yossi, a daughter.

It wasn't Yossi who, in the late 1980s, proposed that they leave and emigrate to Israel. Galina had heard the neighbours going around the town asking who was Jewish. 'Sometimes you can't specify the threat. It's enough to hear the rumours to get you afraid,' she told me.

They studied *The White Book*, a state anti-Zionist publication which described Israel's bloodthirsty wars, how fresh water was brought by camels to Be'ersheva, a propaganda tool to prevent Jews leaving, 'an artful mixture of lies and truth'. During the perestroika period she and Yossi came to Israel on vacation, and in 1990 they left the Soviet Union for good.

Yan had pointed out to her that her son by her first marriage, who was not Jewish, would be conscripted into the army, but it didn't sink in until she received his call-up papers. But even then, she wasn't afraid. 'The Russian army is far more frightening than the Israeli army,' she told me. 'It would offer far worse conditions, the veterans against the youngsters, the cruelty and the brutality.' Had her son not left Russia he would now be fighting Muslims in Chechnya, she pointed out. Instead, at twenty-five, 'he is now the greatest Zionist in the family. In the army there is a term, "poisoned", which means you are crazy about the army and about the country. That's him.' A year after this meeting, her daughter, the half-Jewish child of herself and Yossi, in a civil ceremony on the island of Cyprus married her Irish-Catholic British boyfriend, infatuated with Britain and all things British.

My parents had spent a placid century after leaving eastern Europe. Though they were in some senses people whose lives were thwarted, who belonged neither here nor there, still on what they felt was the wrong side of the Atlantic, nothing much had happened to them, apart from those few years of blitz, when the Liverpool docks were heavily bombed by the Luftwaffe and my father, too old and bronchitic for military service, had pulled the headless corpse of a child from the rubble. History washed over them, like quiet stones undisturbed at the bottom of the river.

Yan and Rosita took me on a wonderful day out on a very cold, very rainy December Saturday, up to the Judean hills, where we visited a vineyard run by Italian Israelis. Another time we drove south, into the desert, to the Nabatean remains, a civilisation of Arab traders I had never even heard of. They talked about their daughter in America, training to be a vet, and whether she would ever return to Israel, given the limited opportunities for employment in her field, and their son, still doing his military service, who, rather late in life, being a shy geeky boy, had finally found a girlfriend. He was taking her on holiday to a five-star hotel in Prague. Rosita feared he would rush into an engagement. They spoke English to me, Russian to each other and Hebrew to their children.

The time I spent with them reminded me that people can get sick to the stomach of history; that too much history can make you want to be sick, especially when it keeps thrashing you around like a fish being whacked against the rocks.

When the power went out in my Tel Aviv apartment one morning, during a heavy storm, Yan told me to check the switch for the heater. 'It's probably shorted in the rain,' he said.

'These Jewish men in Russia,' Rosita told Ilana, the wife of Ophir, 'they were like the masters of the universe. They got the best grades in school and university, they aimed at the best jobs, they were scientists who also read widely in literature and the humanities. Their mothers and wives waited on them hand and foot.'

On the day when Saddam was captured, I spoke to Yan on the phone.

'The Americans of course will try him,' he said, 'but maybe the Iraqis will insist that he's handed over to them. The Iraqis, I think, will be more decisive.'

'I keep forgetting,' I said, 'that you had two years under Stalin.'

But mostly we talked about wine, and good food, and books we had both read, and whether their daughter in America was ever going to meet anyone, and whether their son was going to plunge too soon into marriage with the first girl he met.

Yan's mother, as I write, is slipping into that same place where my own mother had spent her last years, where the memory of the present is dissolving. A place of short, circular conversations with her son, which break his heart. In such cases, only deep memory remains. I wonder what she remembers of the time when she was young, during some of the worst years of that terrible century.

Jooz

There is a particular seductive intimacy in email, which allows people recklessly to reveal themselves, or, if they want, to invent and burnish a new identity. I knew Ophir on the screen of my computer before we ever met. For two months I walked about inside Ophir's marriage, his family, his home, his personal history. People used to write each other letters, which had their own form and conventions, but neither of us would have put all this down on paper and folded it in an envelope with the other's address and taken it to the postbox.

My email exchanges with Ophir, from early January 2003 onwards, created in me a yearning to be there in Israel, a reigniting of the old romance with Tel Aviv. During the Iraq war, which started in the March, I was in contact with him several times a day, and the morning that British Airways announced it was resuming its flights to Tel Aviv now that the military campaign in the Western Desert had been completed and no weapons of mass destruction had been found that could be aimed at Israel, I thought, to hell with it, as my mother used to say when she went out and bought a new dress she couldn't afford – and I booked a ticket. I went to Israel in the middle of the Iraq war because I was deafened by the row about it at home. I was trying to start a novel and I couldn't hear myself think. In Israel the population was not so much for or against the war as worried about whether they would get through it to the end of the day. On the plane flying over, I stared out of the window at the sky, trying to spot anti-aircraft missiles streaking towards us above the gassy mountains of clouds.

I arrived at the airport with the signs above the baggage-claim carousels announcing the location of the nearest air-raid shelter, and there was Ophir to meet me, standing in front of a gift shop in jeans and a blue sweatshirt, and he said, 'You came! Even when the plane landed I didn't quite believe you would be on it.' He has one of those faces that makes him look as if he is always trying to control his urge to start laughing at the absurdity of life, as if he expects the *balaganness* of it to break out at every moment. In one photograph he sent me, of himself in a grey double-breasted suit, standing on the balcony of his apartment just before leaving for a Jewish-Moroccan wedding, he appears as a typical East End wide boy, transported to the hot sun of the Middle East. His wife, Ilana, the doctor, is small, slim and very dark-haired, 'a blackie', he calls her.

We got in his car and drove to an apartment someone had lent me on Ruppin Street, half a block away from the one I would later rent. This one had a long balcony from which you could look down the road opposite, past the Bauhaus buildings, to a short strip of blue. The apartment building was covered with bougainvillea, and palm trees shaded the people who sat out in the late afternoon sunshine, drinking coffee. And next to the bed I had been kindly left a cardboard box containing a gas mask and vial of atropine, the anti-nerve gas agent, just in case.

I think I was the only tourist in the country, apart from the Texan twin giants who had heard the call of the Lord in the Panhandle to travel to Is-re-al to convert the Jews. I had dinner in Jerusalem with David Grossman and his wife Michal. Their young daughter rang in the middle; she was anxious, because of the war, Michal said. The invasion force had not yet taken Baghdad, so who knew how it would all turn out? Maybe they would be repelled by the Ba'athists, just as Saddam had promised. Maybe the Americans would be kicked all the way back to Kuwait and Saddam would be proclaimed the new Saladin and give out more $10,000 cheques to the families of Palestinian suicide bombers? There were endless things to worry about, such as a rumour which had taken hold that a Syrian sleeper agent was abroad in the country with a vial full of anthrax.

When they got home David told his daughter a bedtime story. 'Israel has a tourist, and in her honour the government is going to issue a commemorative coin and a commemorative stamp, which will be called a linda. So you will ask for two lindas for your letter, or ask, have you got change of this linda?'

A few days later Ophir and Ilana decided to take me for a day out. We drove north to the Galilee where I had not been since 1967. We skirted the lake and sat in the café at the kibbutz where, thirty-six years ago, I had learned the minute I set out for the banana plantations on the first morning what a useless specimen of Diaspora humanity I was, passing out after five minutes in the hot sun. I raised my arm and the kibbutz girls screamed; they had never seen shaven armpits before.

Overlooking those lapping waters where I had learned to

swim, having failed numerous times in the municipal swimming pool in Liverpool, we had coffee and I remembered the terrible rows I had with my father when I got back from Israel, after we had been taken up to the newly occupied Golan and bought souvenirs from monumentally polite and smiling Arab stall-holders in Jerusalem's Old City. Rows that had nothing whatsoever to do with the people of this region, their fate, but were entirely about my own rebellion against him, against *his* world and its certainties. 'Israel doesn't have the right to exist,' I shouted. If he had said, 'I agree,' I would have bought an Israeli flag and a pair of shorts, moved to a kibbutz and married a tractor driver.

I didn't try to explain this to Ophir and Ilana. I would have been too embarrassed.

We left the kibbutz and drove up to the Golan Heights, to a restaurant whose tables were set beside a stream. The sound of firing from an army base behind the trees accompanied our lunch. 'What's that?' I asked the waitress. 'Background noise,' she replied, dourly.

A few days later it was Passover. The whole country took to the north–south highway, and me among them, with Ophir, to his mother's cousin in Yavne. 'Can you imagine,' the cousin said to me, 'what it's like to be the mother of three sons in Israel?'

I chatted at length to one of her sons, Oz, an open-faced, bright boy, recently out of the army and the obligatory post-conscription world tour. He was working in a record store, selling and wrapping CDs. He had cut his finger wrapping so many gifts.

We talked about the Iraq war. The men around the table were sceptical. 'This is going to be the Americans' Lebanon,' they said. 'Baghdad will be for them what Beirut was for us.' Oz nodded. He had been in Lebanon, doing things he would not or could not discuss with his parents.

'Look at Dror,' Ophir said, as his daughter arrived with her mother. 'She's wearing eyeshadow.'

'How old is she?'

'Thirteen.'

'She'll have a boyfriend soon.'

'I can't think about that.'

'You're going to have to.'

'Shut up.'

Later that year, when I returned to Israel for my four-month stay, there was a remarkable development in the news: secret peace talks had been conducted, the continuation of the failed talks at Taba (themselves the continuation of the Camp David talks of July 2000) that had terminated, in January 2001, with the vote of no confidence in the then prime minister Ehud Barak and the calling of a general election, won by Ariel Sharon and his right-wing coalition. The participants at Taba, with no mandate either from the Israeli government or the Palestinian Authority, had continued to meet to see if they could come up with an agreement which would have no standing in the political process but which could show both sets of constituents that it was possible to make a deal, one which would, it was hoped, be the template for any future talks.

The accords, which took their name from the city where they were conducted, Geneva, were duly delivered in thick, booklet form to every household in the country. I asked Ophir what he made of them. 'I couldn't wade through all those words,' he said, 'so I just opened up the map at the back, and it looked okay to me.'

The Geneva Accords had settled, once and for all in Ophir's mind, after he had looked at the map and read an all-important paragraph at the front, the only issue that was of interest to him: how the right of return of Palestinian refugees was to be resolved.

If all, or a majority, of refugees returned to the homes from which they had fled or been expelled by Israeli troops in 1948, then within a generation the Jews would be a minority with all that that entailed, having had long and bitter experience of minority status, and on that basis you might as well have asked Ophir what he felt about a peace treaty with the Andromeda Nebula which involved the solar system concession of putting out the sun.

Driving through Israel, he would point out miserable towns, like Hadera, well inside the Green Line, and say, 'The Palestinians can have that one.' Between us, we drew the boundaries of a notional state which consisted of all our favourite bits of Israel, a series of disconnected cantons, distinguished by natural beauty or good shops and restaurants. But his bottom line was that it had to be a Jewish country.

If Yan and Rosita had been formed by their family's violent collision with History in twentieth-century Russia, Ophir came out of his own infernal experience at a minor public school in the England of the 1970s, a personal war with the British and the leftovers of the fag end of the empire – a child's war, seen from a child's height, a playground battle between small-time bullies and causally, pettily, anti-Semitic teachers.

He was an Israeli with a non-Jewish father, an aircraft engineer from Hertfordshire yeoman stock whose career had been spent travelling the world on short-term contracts, working for the aviation industry and foreign governments. He had come to Israel in the early 1960s, when he was helping the Israeli Aircraft Industries build the Arava, an Israeli aircraft used for troop transport of commando units.

Ophir's mother arrived in Israel at the age of five in 1948, from a *Lager* (a holding place for Jews) in Trieste, Italy. Her father had spent most of the war in a Nazi work camp after fleeing the pogroms at Yassi in his home country, Romania. He escaped the camp but was captured by the Russians and sentenced to hard labour in the Gulag, from which he also escaped. He returned to Romania to collect his wife and child (Ophir's mother) and from there they escaped again, this time by foot, his second son born on the way. They spent the rest of the war in Vienna, where his third son was born. They were living on false papers and he was earning a living as a trader, dealing in anything he could get his hands on, from cigarettes to nylons and gold. He was able to weigh gold accurately in the palm of his hand till the day he died.

The family were fortunate to have blond hair and blue eyes, and could pass as non-Jews. When the war ended, they joined the rest of the displaced, and were transported to the Italian refugee camp.

'My grandfather,' Ophir said, 'was never comfortable with the refugee status and preferred to make his own living. He got caught smuggling Luckies and other contraband black-market goodies across the lines to the Russkies, and was thrown in the slammer. Only Grandma's quick wit and natural linguistic abilities with the American camp officers got him out of the mess, in a prisoner-exchange deal. They were told they could go to America or Israel. My grandfather said America. For the first time in her life, my grandmother stood against him and said Israel – she was not ever going to live at the beck and call, generosity and mercy of a goy ever again. He bent at her adamant insistence. He never regretted it.

'My grandfather was a huge man with massively strong, shovel-like hands. After they arrived in Israel he was drafted into the fledgling Israeli Defence Force (IDF) in 1948, and later fought again in the battle against the Jordanian Legion, taking the police station at Latroun on the way to Jerusalem. During the Six Day War the three of them, my uncles and himself, each fought at a different front. He was never a good socialist, although he blindly voted for Mapai [Labour] all of his life. He was a natural businessman, always his own man. He built up a building business with an Iraqi-born partner that lasted over thirty-five years and employed Ramle Arabs. He was always darker tanned than his Iraqi partner, and spoke better Arabic too.'

Ophir's mother went to work first for IAI, then El Al, running its airport VIP service, and met the young English engineer, married him and later moved with him to Hertfordshire where their two sons would grow up, spending every summer in Israel with their grandparents.

When Ophir was eleven, the family moved from Dunstable to St Albans, where he started at school. I had also gone to an English school where Israel was still called Palestine, where the Empire was only reluctantly giving way in the minds of the teachers to the Commonwealth, where the Jewish girls were separated out on our parents' insistence from morning prayers so our mouths would not have to be contaminated by the name of Jesus. There was a Jewish girl who was a scapegoat, fat, bespectacled, not even academically bright, the friendless one whom everyone picked on, and it was later suggested to me, in adulthood, by one of the non-Jewish girls, that perhaps it was motivated by anti-Semitism. I was one of those who picked on her, and maybe I was trying to cleanse myself of guilt by association.

But this was insignificant stuff; girls can be cruel and heartless to those they select as outsiders. Ophir was locking his horns against what he thought of as a whole system. It started at once, he said, with the geography teacher, 'who we used to call Bullet, who had a map on the wall where Israel appeared as Palestine and to my face he called Jews and Israelis "terrorist wogs". When I objected, to the headmaster, I was told that this was a traditional school and these kinds of attitudes would take a long time to filter out. Israel was a young country and who knew if it would still be around, so why change the maps?'

As for calling Jews 'wogs', Ophir was to understand that there was nothing derogatory in the term, it simply meant Western Oriental Gentleman, an explanation that had already been delivered to arriving immigrants from India and Pakistan, who were equally sceptical about its intentions towards the people it addressed, and now the term 'wog' struggles to find a final squalid corner in the English language inside the mouths of the older members of the far right and other racist organisations.

In 1976, the PLO hijacked an Air France plane bound for Tel Aviv and diverted it to Entebbe airport, in Uganda. The non-Jewish passengers were released and one hundred and five Jews and Israelis were taken hostage. The Israeli air force mounted a well-planned and well-executed raid on the plane and freed them, the first time that a foreign government had undertaken an exercise against terrorism outside its own borders. It was a really good time to be an Israeli; the Entebbe incident reinforced an image of Jews they had been trying to cement since 1967 – of lightning-quick operations involving a combination of brains and *chutzpah*.

'I was feeling quite good about myself,' Ophir said, 'because a member of my family took part in that escapade. My mother had brought back this El Al bag for me in the Israeli colours and since everybody in the news was talking about Entebbe, this cheeky little thing the Jews did, I was going to carry this El Al bag instead of one with Adidas or Norwich City football club on it.

'A few wankers took offence and one day they ambushed me on the way to school. Six of them beat the crap out of me fifty yards from the school gate. They said to me, "We thought you people were heroes. How come you didn't beat *us* up?" No one came to help the cheeky fucker with the El Al bag. I went to the school nurse and she took me to the head and said it was anti-Semitism, but he said that I bore some responsibility for displaying the bag and, anyway, no one had witnessed it, so he couldn't do too much. He said I should keep a low profile and use an English name instead of my Hebrew name.

'I decided that if I was going to get nothing out of the school I was going to deal with the situation in another way, and beat the crap out of those six wankers as individuals, myself. I was thirteen, I'd just got laid for the first time, and I ended up targeting them one by one, but funnily enough, I did it with no one else looking and when I was called to the head's office I got punished. He said he had to act because the parents had complained. I said, "You didn't punish them when I complained," and he said, "That's different."

'All sorts of shit went on in those years. Every time I got into a fight I defended myself. I told them it was against my religion to turn the other cheek. This wanker started spray-painting signs saying "Jews Out". He said, "We're doing it for the best, you're having such a hard time, you don't belong here." He came at me and whacked me in the face and there was a cricket bat nearby so I smacked him on the arse with it. The teacher came in and told me that Christian values were not as barbaric as Jewish ones. "We don't give an eye for an eye and a tooth for a tooth." He told me Judaism was a primitive culture that had no business being in his school, where Christianity had evolved to turning the other cheek.'

As soon as he graduated from university, Ophir left Britain and returned to the country of his birth. He served in the Israeli air force, a desk job, selling off air force surplus.

He didn't think of himself as a Zionist, he wasn't interested in isms and ologies. His mind didn't work that way. 'As far as I'm

concerned, Zionism is dead,' he wrote to me. 'It served its purpose and is now (over fifty years) obsolete. It's a yearning word,
a movement word that has run its course, just like "next year in
Jerusalem". I can point to the moment the word became obsolete. It was in 1948 with the declaration of an independent
state – ISRAEL. Zion was not chosen as the name of the re-
incarnated home of the Jooz – and that's symbolic enough for
me. We can leave the word's ownership and use to the new anti-
Semites, who use it extensively to shield and hide behind their
real agenda. I'm not a Zionist, I'm an Israeli – now try to fucking
bully me around.'

Ophir and his younger brother Dror (after whom his daughter
would be named) were fourteen months apart in age. 'He was
built like a brick shithouse,' Ophir said, 'and with it, he was also
possibly the most naive person I ever knew, and also the most
generous, even with my money.'

Dror avoided the anti-Semitism of Ophir's upbringing simply
by going to a different school, an ordinary comprehensive where
the maps showed the world as it was, not as it had been. Every
summer the two boys would go to stay with their grandparents in
Israel and in his early teens Dror told his mother he wasn't
coming back to Hertfordshire. He persuaded them to enrol him
in an Israeli boarding school. Later he returned to England to
finish his education, but he never felt he belonged and was soon
on his way back to Israel.

Ophir didn't think Dror would do well in the Israeli army.
'There's a saying that if you piss on the IDF, they get wet, but if
the IDF pisses on you, you drown. I thought Dror was going to
have a hard time.' But Dror had made up his mind and, through
his uncle's contacts, got himself a place in the paratroopers.
'They called him Horse. When you go on troop marches, someone has to carry a stretcher and someone has to carry 40 kilos of

water, and someone has to carry the MAG [a 30-calibre machine gun], and someone has to carry a radio. Well, my brother adopted the MAG as his own and wouldn't let anyone else carry it, so he would carry the MAG, and the water, and would take one end of the stretcher. He expanded on army food, his neck expanded. He enjoyed the army, the red beret of the paratroopers, everything.'

Dror had returned to Israel in 1983, during the Lebanon war, and got shipped out there right away. 'There was all kinds of crazy shit going on,' Ophir said. 'There was a lot of collecting of ears off Syrian troop bodies, a whole macho thing going, they were fucking around with all kinds of experimental weapons. And there was my brother going round with a huge pain in his abdomen and they brought him back to see a doctor, who told him it was back pain and he shouldn't carry so much. It got to the point where the pain was unbearable and now he had a lump on his neck. That's when I told my officer friend and she got him to a major army medical unit and they diagnosed him with teratoma, testicular cancer.

'We took him back to London for treatment. He had chemo for a year, by which time he looked less like a hulk and more like a skeleton with a nine-month pregnant woman's abdomen. Yet we were always optimistic, he was a huge man who wasn't going to give in, he should have been dead by now so that meant he was going to continue to fight it. Then Dror said he didn't want to be in England any more, he wanted to go home to Israel.

'He was a decimated person, someone else. The way it ended, the growth was squeezing his kidney and his blood was being poisoned. The night he died I saw that he was not himself any more, even though he was still fighting. I walked up to him and whispered, "It's okay, you can sleep now," and a minute later, he died. And that was the end of it. He was twenty-one. He was buried here in Israel and this is why I am here and why I will never leave.

'When we were kids, any time anyone said something to Dror, he always said he wouldn't believe it unless he checked with me, and whenever anyone asked him what he was going to do with his life he said it didn't matter because "my brother Ophir is going to do it all", and the day he died I lost my motivation because there wasn't anyone to do it for. I didn't want to become a millionaire any more. My family was going to be my big success. But the funny thing was, he didn't need me for anything. When we were kids he'd be in town and I'd get a call from him. He'd say, these guys have pinned me down, get on your skateboard and get over here. Then he'd proceed to wipe out three or four guys while I stood there and watched. I never understood why he needed me. Maybe it was that I was the brains and he was the hands. But it wasn't a waste, his life, he did what he wanted and through him I met Ilana and married her, with his blessing.'

She worked enormously long hours as a paediatrician at the Tel Hashomer hospital in Tel Aviv. She showed me round the intensive-care ward and explained how they would be treating a child in one bed whose arm was blown off in a terrorist attack, and next to her a boy from Gaza with a rare medical condition. She introduced me to the volunteer social worker, a bearded religious man, who had a lot of tricky problems to deal with. The kid from Gaza's parents were locked in inside the checkpoints and couldn't get permits to travel outside that strip of land which was now a giant open-air prison, so the hospital social worker had to find relatives inside Israel who could act *in loco parentis*.

Ilana was born in Vilnius, in Lithuania. The family, who were doctors, like Yan and Rosita's parents, left in 1973, when she was eight years old. She described the cruelty of the playground anti-Semitism, the viciousness of the teachers towards her, 'and the one who was the worst was a Jew herself,' she said. She couldn't remember a word of Lithuanian. She had cut that portion of her life out of herself. Even her name was changed, from Elina.

I think that Ilana thought Ophir was a big kid, an adolescent who never grew up, but after seventeen years of marriage and two children, the intimacy of their relationship is still visible in the hands they hold, walking down the street. I have never met a better matched couple. He would hang out with his friend Fatachalla, a Palestinian-Israeli who ran a construction company in the Arab village of Qalansuwa. They walked along the beach together, and their wives, though they never met, Ilana in her turquoise hospital overalls, Tagrid in her hijab, rolled their eyes at the total nonsense these feckless husbands talked.

After many years of working as the CEO of a high-tech start-up, when Ilana was promoted to a management position in the Israeli health-care system, she made him give up his job and do something else, because his stress levels were going to kill him, she said. Emails started to arrive in my inbox with a little logo at the bottom of two heads, rotating round each other. He had gone in for life coaching, with a specialisation in conflict resolution.

He told me this in a café at Heathrow airport on a six-hour stopover from a summer in Seattle.

'What? You?'

'I'm a good listener,' he said.

And it was true, he was. In life he was silent, only on the pixels of the screen did he expose the raw flesh of all that pain.

Secretly, he was writing prose-poetry, in the style of the great Israeli poet Yehuda Amichai. He was trying to pay homage to something, to family, to what it took to survive and the various strategies people had for doing it.

My grandfather's skin, was plowed and engraved, unnaturally like the alien misplaced fields in the Negev desert. He bent a lot, like flexible tall grass in the strong wind, while the hard trees around him resisted and broke. His sons faced the wind side on, collecting less resistance, feet planted in the ground, their heads in the clouds, diverting the wind like fins, they made use of its power.

Uprooted in strange land, I smelt the diverted wind, it carried an unfamiliar smell, a rich organic mix of unknown love, yet unquestioning, I associated it with home and followed. Instinctively bending in the storm I buried my face in the soil, letting the wind press me closer, reacquainting myself. I scratched at the soil and plowed myself in with my feet, planting my hands in deep I could not feel the buffeting of the storm.

They live in Rannana, a dormitory town north of Tel Aviv. The deputy mayor has the idea of making a zoo there, importing bears from Africa. 'The idiot doesn't realise there are no bears in Africa,' Ophir said. Ilana and her mother-in-law found the apartment. 'I wasn't allowed to have anything to do with it. They made the decision for me.' It is in a very nice suburban community, rather soulless for my taste, but ideal for children, with bridges across the quiet roads so the kids won't run into traffic.

Last time I was there, his daughter Dror was keeping a rabbit. 'It's having a kid,' her brother Tom said, cradling it in his arms.

'She won't let him touch it when she's home,' Ophir said. 'Dror terrifies me.'

'Why?'

'She's a woman.'

'What about Tom?'

'He's mine.'

'What happens when it's time for him to go into the army?'

'He's not going. My family has given enough.'

'What does Ilana say?'

'You'll have to ask her.'

But she would just give me a smile behind his back, because she knew that boys don't grow up as fast as girls, they're big kids all their lives, and when it comes to what they are expected to do in this country, maybe it's a mercy that they get to play as long as they can.

Davka

From: Linda Grant

Sent: 31 January 2005 23:13

To: [various]

Subject: davka

Dear Israeli friend

I am conducting an investigation into the meaning and usages of the word 'davka', which has no English equivalent and is possibly an essential aspect of Israeliness. I would be grateful if you could provide me with an example of a sentence using this word, such as: 'There are 50 items on the menu, but davka, they don't have the one I want.'

There will be a prize. It is a pair of special 3D glasses that turn Christmas into Chanukah, purchased at the Jewish Community Centre, Washington DC, and used, very effectively, on the giant Christmas tree at Rockefeller Plaza, New York City, proving, as we knew all along, that the anti-Semites are right and it's really Jew York.

I look forward to your reply.

Best wishes

Linda Grant

From: Daphna Baram

Sent: 01 February 2005 01:46

To: Linda Grant

Subject: Re: davka

Interesting. My friends in the army used to call me Davka, because it sounds a bit like Daphna, and because they claimed it goes well with my personality (my high school friends used to call me Bafla under a similar pretext).

The word davka has various uses, and I'll try and demonstrate a few of them.

Benign: 'I thought it would be a terribly boring party but davka it was nice.'

Stubborn or spiteful: 'I was in a hurry and was late for my meeting so she davka took her time and spent an hour in the shower.'

Different grammatic use: 'He was being all nice and charming and wanted to take me out for some fancy dinner, but I've done a davka on him and stayed at home sulking.' (In Hebrew: 'asiti lo davka.')

Contemporary: 'The fact that he says that he is the enemy of racism and

Fascism wherever they are davka proves that he is actually an enemy of Israel and therefore an anti-Semite.'

I think I qualify for the kind of glasses which turn Hanuka into Christmas, but keeps the jelly donuts and latkes in it.

D x

From: Ophir Wright

Sent: 01 February 2005 06:39

To: Linda Grant

Subject: Re: davka

'You're not going to tell me who to marry, I'm davka marrying the shikse.'

'Out of all the fine Jewish girls in the world, you davka had to find a shikse.'

'You know, having met the shikse, she's davka a mensch.'

'You bitch, did you have to davka bang my best mate.'

'I'll do it davka, just to spite you, hoe bitch . . .'

A Jewish Bogart would have said, 'Of all the bars, in all the world, you davka had to walk into this one . . .'

Ophir

From: Eric Silver

Sent: 01 February 2005 07:10

To: Linda Grant

Subject: Re: davka

Hi Linda

I think davka is Aramaic. My favourite definition is an Israeli driving the wrong way down a one-way street – on purpose.

Luv, Eric

From: Yan

Sent: 01 February 2005 07:22

To: Linda Grant

Subject: davka contest

Hi there

I shall enter the contest, probably. A remark re the following: 'There are 50 items on the menu, but davka, they don't have the one I want.'

'But' does not go with 'davka', it is just not necessary. In Hebrew, the sentence will look approximately like this: 'These momzers have 50 items on the menu, davka gefilte fish is out!'

Another use of 'davka' – somebody does (to you) something opposite of the expected/desired. Children use it frequently in the following way: 'I asked him to lend me his bicycle for a ride, and this bastard has done davka. Slapped me a few, too.'

Yan

From: David Passow

Sent: 01 February 2005 08:20

To: Linda Grant

Subject: Re: davka

Dear Linda

Davka is an Aramaic word (long before Israelis) which means 'it so happens' or 'it so happens that precisely . . .' Like so many terms from a different language, the nuance is almost as important as the literal meaning. Does this help?

Regards, David Passow

From: Etgar Keret

Sent: 02 February 2005 14:30

To: Linda Grant

Subject: Re: davka

Hi Linda

I went for a Polish mother-style sentence: 'I davka liked your old haircut much better.'

(: Etgar

From: R. Domb

Sent: 05 February 2005 13:16

To: Linda Grant

Subject: Re: davka

Dear Linda

I could spend ages on researching 'our davka' as it is referred to in a Hebrew Book for Beginners. However, it seems to me that the example you gave is a 'Yiddish davka', whereas Israelis use it more in a negative or defiant way: 'I davka love him' means that he is not really worthy of love but nevertheless I love him. Well, I could go on, but you probably had by now inspired examples so I look forward to read one day what you wrote about it. Etgar will probably come up with something amusing.

Lehitraot, Risa

From: Hillels

Sent: 06 February 2005 12:50

To: Linda Grant

Subject: davka

Davka?! Well, let's see.

As a sample sentence, how about, 'I wanted his help, and he did me a davka' (i.e., he did the opposite of what I wanted).

I don't know why, but if I examine myself, I haven't used the term lately, and I haven't heard it used by others that much either. These things are either In or Out — for those of us who are, consciously or unconsciously, Dedicated Followers of Fashion (the Kinks, right?). Or maybe it's just a question of personality.

Is it an essential aspect of Israeliness? Davka, I'm not sure.

By the way, in the late 60s, New Left pro-Israel progressive Jews in the States actually published a periodical called Davka, I believed based in California. If I'm not mistaken, the editor was Aaron Manheimer.

One of your Israeli friends, Hillel

From: Linda Grant

Sent: 06 February 2005 20:21

To: [various]

Subject: Results of the davka contest

Dear Israeli friend

I am pleased to announce the final results of the davka contest. Thank you for your entry, if you entered.

First prize, of a pair of 3D glasses that turn Christmas into Chanukah, goes to Ophir Wright of Rannana, Israel for his simple, elegant entry which inserted the word into a well-known phrase or saying: 'Of all the bars in all the world, she davka had to walk into mine.'

Highly commended: Etgar Keret, of Tel Aviv, Israel, who entered what he described as a Polish mother davka which rendered some of the complex malevolence of the word: 'I davka liked your old haircut much better.'

Honorable mention to Daphna Baram of Oxford who pointed out that she davka was the kind of person who preferred a pair of X-ray glasses that turned Chanukah into Christmas.

Thank you to David Passow of Jerusalem and Eric Silver, also of Jerusalem, for identifying the word as coming from the Aramaic.

Best wishes

Linda Grant

From: Ophir Wright

Sent: 07 February 2005 06:14

To: Linda Grant

Subject: Re: Results of the davka contest

I'm davka pleased with the outcome of this.

Thanks.

From: Judah Passow

Sent: 06 February 2005 22:21

To: Linda Grant

Subject: Re: Results of the davka contest

Rick's (Bogart) line in the scene is actually 'Of all the gin joints in all the towns in all the world, she walks into mine.'

J.

From: Eric Silver

Sent: 07 February 2005 06:15

To: Linda Grant

Subject: Re: Results of the davka contest

Thanks. Shouldn't it be 'gin joints'?

Eric.

From: Yan

Sent: 07 February 2005 07:05

To: Linda Grant

Cc: Ophir Wright

Subject: Results of the davka contest

In the best traditions of any rotten liberal democracy, I PROTEST!

The grounds for this PROTEST are:

1. The original invitation was sent to my work mail, against the regulations (as the mail with the results, too), and I just plain forgot to submit my entries.

2. Mr Wright is cheating! I can't prove it yet, but I feel it in my waters. You just wait till I find the source of his entry. Then it is 10 years of litigation.

3. I was busy.

4. How do you like them 1–3?

Cheers, Yan

From: Ophir Wright

Sent: 07 February 2005 08:08

To: Yan; Linda Grant

Subject: Re: Results of the davka contest

To your item number one – mere technicality. You admit freely that you received the invitation. So, we can assume that you were either malingering away from work, or that you had jumped on this as a prepared excuse for not participating.

As to your item number two, I say ignorance of the classics (is no excuse). I made the judge fully aware that my contribution was based on Bogart's classic line. In fact, not many know that he was actually Jewish. In rehearsals, he just couldn't refrain from placing the word 'davka' in that most famous of lines (but it was edited out by the anti-Semite director). It fit the bill and the scene, which depicted the flight of two Jews escaping Nazi, and more importantly French (may their nation be wiped from the face of the earth) persecution. Rick (Bogart) in this scene davka chooses to go against his own self-preservation, and love for a woman, which if you think about it results in a Double Davka.

Your item number three borders on the pathetic and brings to the surface your 'bad loser' complex.

Item number four prompts me to note that in your entire protest appeal, you didn't use the word 'davka' once, which confirms my previously noted diagnosis of Latent Loser disorder. I would suggest that before you carry on with the rest of your life, do at least one of the following: consult with Mr Peres, who's worked out a comfort zone for his loser streak, and stop reading all those fucking intellectual books you're into. Get in front of the box, you might learn something of real value.

And finally, davka because you are a loser, I love you.

Ophir

From: Judah Passow

Sent: 07 February 2005 09:19

To: Linda Grant

Subject: Re: Results of the davka contest

Not only were Casablanca's writers anything but anti-Semitic – they were very much Jewish. The script was written by the Epstein Brothers (Phil and Julius) and Howard Koch (subsequently blacklisted during the McCarthy era for being part of the Jewish/communist conspiracy in Hollywood). The film has davka an unimpeachable Jewish pedigree – the screenplay is based on an unproduced script for a play called 'Everybody Comes To Rick's', written in 1940 by Murray Bennett, a Jewish school teacher from New York. Hal Wallis (born Harold Wallis in Chicago to Jewish immigrant parents) bought the script for Warner Brothers and produced the film. He gave the director's job to Mike Curtiz, who of course was born Mihaly Kertesz in Hungary, the son of a prosperous Jewish family.

Why and how do I know all this? I spent four years sitting in a small screening theater on Commonwealth Avenue in Boston watching everything made in Hollywood between 1938 and 1956 and everything made in France between 1965 and 1969. I then wrote a senior thesis entitled 'The Origins of Cinema Vérité Camerawork in Film Noir', which resulted in my being instantly hired by NBC as a cameraman and fired by them five months later when they got sick and tired of my evening news footage looking like out-takes from a Godard film all the time.

Judah

From: Ophir Wright

Sent: 07 February 2005 10:02

To: Linda Grant

Subject: Re: Results of the davka contest

GOD almighty, I was just being sarcastic and mixing fact and bullshit. I shudder at the thought that a huge distribution list of people will read it.

As far as J's historical review is concerned, made my day really, what with all those Jooz involved.

Ophir

From: Daphna Baram

Sent: 07 February 2005 11:04

To: Linda Grant

Subject: Re: Results of the davka contest

Thank you, I'm honored to be on the honorary list, and think that Ophir won his glasses by right. I was also surprised to learn that Etgar knows my mother. I'll have to investigate this next time I go home.

I'm very curious to know what you are up to, but I'll wait patiently, and will just send you davka anecdotes whenever I get any. Last week I made a vain attempt to translate the concept, and called a friend of mine in an email Anshel 'to spite' Pfeffer. He was very offended and said that he doesn't mind being called 'davka', but that 'to spite', so he said, 'implies that I am a bad person'. He is English so I'm taking his word for it and will never attempt to play games with davka again . . .

D.

Pigua

Edited version of interview with the speaker, November 2003.

'Me, Yossi Mendelevich, I was considered to be a very protective father. But there was a hole in my plan, I let my son take buses. I'm going to show you everything that happened on the last day of my son Yuval's life, which was 5 March 2003, when he was thirteen and a half years old, so you will understand the banality of the atrocity. At 6.45am I woke him up, he hugged me and said, give me some strength for the morning, so I hugged him strongly. He got up, he washed his face, brushed his teeth, ate Cocoa Pops and milk for breakfast and picked up a cheese sandwich his mother had made him for lunch.

'While he was waking up here in Haifa his murderer Mohammed Kwassama was travelling back from Hebron, where he had picked up the bomb, to Abu Dis where they are now building the fence, but there was no fence there then and no one stopped him at the checkpoint. Around 11am when Yuval was finishing maths, the murderer was arriving in Haifa. He decided to wait until 2pm when all the kids from school were going home and the buses were more crowded. At 2.05pm Yuval got on the 37 bus here, at the stop by his school, sat down on the fifth row, right behind the murderer, and at 2.07pm the bus started moving. After driving three hundred metres he rang his mother to let her know he was on his way home. After this traffic light, at 2.10pm, Yuval rang me. He told me he was a little late because his art teacher had asked him to stay on after school to make a paper lion for Purim. I told him a joke, he laughed, he said, "Daddy, I love you" and at that moment, 2.14pm and 32 seconds, according to the time the watch stopped on his wrist, the murderer activated the detonator of the belt carrying 17lb of explosives, along with hundreds of small metal balls designed to worsen the impact. The bomb was made by a master of such diabolic devices in Hebron, Ali Alan, who has now been killed by Israeli security forces.

   'When the phone went dead I thought it was only a disturbance in the cellular system and I didn't get suspicious. Then I got a call from a friend who said, "How is Yuval?" I said, "Why?" He said, "You heard there was a suicide bomb in Moriah Avenue?" I was shivering, a cold sweat was on my skin. Our house is three kilometres away. I drove down the street and saw the bus. You can see here exactly where it blew up and over there on that part of the road is where they laid the bodies in black and blue body bags. Moriah is the name of the mountain where God tested Abraham to sacrifice his son Isaac but no one called from the sky to save my boy.

   'There was a smell of burned flesh in the air and I thought of Yuval's great-grandparents who were wiped from the earth in

Poland in 1941. That was their holocaust, this is his. Now I want to show you the wall here behind the bus stop, where the blood of our children was spilled. Seventeen people were massacred that day, a Druze, a Muslim Arab, a girl of the Bahai faith. Exactly two weeks before Yuval was murdered, he participated in a co-existence project in an Arab village. This was bi-national Haifa. My barber, our butcher, our grocer are all Arab. Seven thousand people came to our house in the days of mourning, but no Arabs came. That is a devastating issue for me. Meanwhile, in Abu Dis the family of Mohammed Kwassama were holding three days of celebration. He was not a refugee, his house was not demolished. He was a computer student in the Islamic Polytechnic of Hebron. His father works for the municipality as a language teacher. Nothing brought him to that deed but religious ideology.

'This is our house. This is Yuval's room. He loved *Harry Potter* and *Lord of the Rings*. Here is his Nintendo, his dartboard, his guitar, his clothes, his trainers; here is the paper lion he stayed behind at school to make. Did you see this sticker on his door? It says, "A whole generation wants peace" but he changed it to "A whole Yuval wants peace". I am an engineer, not a humanities person. However deep I go into language, I have no words to describe the agony. Some major part of yourself is a black hole. Now we are at the cemetery which overlooks the sea. Here is his grave in the section that the municipality set aside for the victims of terror. It is filling up quite quickly. Here is Yuval Mendelevich under a granite stone, his time in the world, 10.9.198 – 5.3.2003.'

Sarut bamoach

Apart from my dead uncle Hershel, also known as Harry, buried in an Italian graveyard on the Arno river since 1943, who had jumped out of a tank, probably to light a cigarette, and been shot through the head, there were no warriors in my immediate family.
My father was bronchitic and served instead with the Liverpool home guard, defending the docks from the Luftwaffe. His father had worn the uniform of the tsar's army reluctantly, and had fled Poland to avoid reconscription. I never saw a gun or a knife or anyone I knew in battledress. Fighting wasn't for us. We didn't have the physique or the hand–eye coordination. We were too klutzy to kill anyone on purpose.
Yesterday, looking for an old photograph, I found a letter from my father written in the winter of 1961 on his first trip to Israel, on the headed notepaper of the Accadia Hotel, Tel Aviv, and

addressed to my mother, my sister and myself. Reporting on the sights he had seen on a breathless one-day tour of Tel Aviv, Jaffa and Jerusalem, he closed with his most important news: 'Daddy saw the home of the Prime Minister Ben Gurion, a Jewish soldier was on guard.' I don't know what religion or ethnicity he expected the soldier to be, but the sight of a Jewish soldier guarding the home of a Jewish prime minister in a Jewish country was more than his mind could take in, because he breaks off, having reached the end of the page, and doesn't take advantage of the other side of the sheet.

My cousin once suggested that my father was older than he said he was, that lacking a Polish birth certificate (which many years later he tried unsuccessfully to obtain from the Polish embassy in London), his parents had knocked off a few years when declaring him to the British authorities to avoid conscription in the First World War, which ended when he was supposed to be fourteen. There was a tendency to regard soldiering as risking your life over someone else's business, whose interests didn't necessarily coincide with your own. Apart from the Second World War, there wasn't a war that my parents supported, not Vietnam, not the Falklands.

So here is my father confronted with a Jewish soldier. Not an Israeli soldier, he's still getting over the fact that Ben Gurion is being guarded by a Jew with a gun.

My parents believed that Israeli soldiers were all nice Jewish boys who had, by sheer willpower, managed to shoehorn their capacious minds into the narrow fit of the military mentality. They could get their heads round the idea of a Jewish general, planning the logistics of an invasion, but a Jewish private who could shoot straight was a miracle all by itself.

When I first saw the photograph of the ten-year-old Mohammed al Durra cowering against a bullet-pocked wall in

Gaza, sheltering in the arms of his father who could not protect him, when I looked at those frozen frames of the very few seconds left to him of his life, before a bullet or bullets entered his body and he was killed, I did not have an immediate emotional reaction.

My response was the same a year later when the planes flew into the World Trade Center. Shock, but reason was still trying to make sense of it, to order these events, to ask, 'What the fuck is going on?' And the same again when I first saw the torture photographs from Abu Ghraib prison. An Israeli friend told me that in his gut he did not want it to be an Israeli bullet, or bullets, that had killed Mohammed al Durra; it was possible, he believed, that the child had been accidentally shot by Palestinian crossfire, but we would probably never know.

But still you are left with the image of a child cowering against a wall in the middle of a gun battle in which the overwhelming force of arms is on one side. And you are also left with a number, which is that of the total of Palestinian minors under the age of eighteen killed during the intifada: 646.* That number, and the picture, remain long after you have asked all the fruitless questions and received no satisfactory answers. It will never leave you. The child's terror is yours, you knew it long before he did, when you let go of your mother's hand in a crowd and lost sight of her and the alien world swallowed you up. But it was just for a few moments, then she found you. Still, you don't forget those seconds of horror, they are with you all your life.

Mohammed al Durra would soon become a poster, then a postage stamp, and also a poem, by the British poet Tom Paulin,

*According to the statistics collected by the Israeli human rights organisation, B'tselem, as of May 2005.

published in the *Observer* newspaper, in which the child was gunned down by the 'Zionist SS' caught 'in that weasel word "Crossfire".

The living boy became the dead boy and his corpse was dragged through the news pages and the internet, and people insisted that the death was a Palestinian stunt, and others that the Israelis had a policy of shooting kids and were natural born child-killers, and the anti-Semites rushed in with their resurrection of the blood libel, and were countered by lengthy articles about ballistics evidence, or that the child whose body had been driven through the streets of Gaza to his grave was another boy altogether. And eighteen months later, it all started up again when an International Solidarity Movement activist from Seattle, Rachel Corrie, was crushed to death by a bulldozer, and some people said the soldier drove straight at her and killed her for pleasure and others that he couldn't possibly have seen her.

In Tel Aviv, people did not sit round in cafés talking about Mohammed al Durra and Rachel Corrie. When I mentioned the child's name, few people recognised it, though they remembered the photograph only because of the international attention it received. It got inside-page coverage in the Israeli press.

The child had become a symbol, as the photograph of the Jewish boy, around the same age, in little overcoat and cap, raising his hands in front of a Nazi, was the emblem of Jewish suffering in the Shoah. Mohammed al Durra was that Jewish child for millions of people in the Arab and Muslim world, and for those others of different faiths or none, who opened their newspapers in October 2000 and saw it.

Why not for the Israelis?

Because they had their own photograph, taken twelve days after Mohammed al Durra's death. It was not of a child but of a man, a Palestinian in Ramallah raising his bloody hands exultantly to an ecstatic crowd below. The blood was that of two Russian-Israeli off-duty army reservists (or undercover spies, recruiting potential collaborators, according to the Palestinians), who had wandered down the wrong alley and been arrested by the Palestinian police and taken to the police station where a mob stormed the building and lynched them, watched by a cheering crowd of between one and two thousand people. Their bodies were almost too mutilated for recognition (it was rumoured that their brains and liver were torn out and placed in their hands), and one was thrown from the window and chained to the bumper of a car and dragged through the streets of the city.

Barbarim, said my friends in Tel Aviv. Barbarians.

What is the death of soldier (even off-duty) of an occupying army, walking in occupied territory, against the death of a little boy, screaming in terror in his father's arms? Where is the equivalence?

But the Israelis did not see soldiers as we see soldiers. They did not see a helmet and a gun and webbing and boots; they saw their father or their brother or their husband or their son or themselves, because everyone had served in the army, and it was not a career or a place where a society sent the boys for whom it can't find jobs in an age of derelict factories and a limited demand for unskilled, grunting labour.

The soldiers who were murdered in Ramallah were the same Jewish boys my father had seen guarding the house of the prime minister, that miracle of new post-war Jewish life, a Jew with a gun. And for me, less prone to innocent marvelling (as a taxi driver en route from the airport to Jerusalem would show me, bursting with pride, 'the beautiful lights on the highway and the beautiful tanks in the tanks museum, over there, on that beautiful hill'), it was a question of wondering what was going on inside the minds of the soldiers who stood facing Mohammed al Durra and all the other 646 dead Palestinian kids, with guns in their hands, their faces well hidden behind their metal helmets.

I wanted to meet soldiers, to find out what they thought and felt, because one thing I was sure of, they were not metal men, not Terminators, manufactured in a Negev factory out of cyber-energised spare tank parts, but flesh and blood.

A few days after I arrived in Tel Aviv in October 2003 I left the apartment on Ruppin Street and went to an army base near Nablus with Judah Passow. We drove north to Kfar Saba, a prosperous small dormitory town near Rannana where Ophir and Ilana lived. I was navigating. The map showed that if we turned left *here* the road would take us across the Green Line to the West Bank. But when you got to the place where the road should be, it simply curved round again and you got back where you started. We drove for forty-five minutes in circles. The road signs were no help; vandals had painted over the names of the Palestinian cities and only the large settlement of Ariel was marked. We stopped people and asked for directions to the settlement of Kdumim where the soldiers were encamped, but no one we asked had heard of it. Across the Green Line was another country, nobody went there, they didn't think about it, it was perfectly possible to pretend that it did not exist – not just the Palestinian towns but also the Jewish settlements. Before the intifada, Israelis went to the West Bank to eat good food and buy cheap clothes, but since the lynching of the soldiers, almost no one set foot in the West Bank or Gaza unless they lived there, or they were in uniform.

In the end we stopped at a gas station and showed the map to the attendants, who looked at it and explained that it was an optimistic map, an Oslo map, it was a road map that hoped one day highways would be built between two neighbours living in peace, side by side, but in the meantime there was no way that you could get to the West Bank from Kfar Saba, even though it looked the most direct and obvious route. The roads between the two did not exist. They petered out as dead ends.

So we had to ring the captain from the IDF spokesperson's office and get him to guide us in.

The suburbs of the coastal plain stop suddenly, and the dry landscape of the interior replaces them. There is a roadblock, with soldiers checking ID, and a bus stop at which settlers wait for Israeli settler buses that take them to their homes. 'KILL THE AMALEK', someone had scrawled on the bus shelter. In the Bible, when the children of Israel escaped from bondage in Egypt and wandered for forty years in the desert, the stragglers at the back, the old, the feeble, the very young, were picked off by the savage tribe of the Amalek, and since then Jews have been enjoined to decimate the Amalek wherever they found them, but since no one knows any more who the Amalek are (having adopted deep cover), the ruling is in abeyance. For some of the settlers of the West Bank, the Palestinians were the Amalek, and it was their God-given duty to kill them. Judaism, in Israel, had created a radical far-right fringe of religious fundamentalists, typical of radical fundamentalists everywhere, who identify the enemy and loudly call for their elimination. Sometimes I thought that the Jewish extremists and the Islamic extremists should be given their own state, the borders sealed, and then the rest of us could let them get on with the job of annihilating each other and we could be left in peace. One fascist, and I'm quite prepared to call him that, Baruch Goldstein, had in 1994 entered the mosque in Hebron and gunned down twenty-nine Palestinians at prayer. Hamas and Islamic Jihad responded with attacks on buses in Israel. Tit for tat. Tat tat tat.

We drove along a settler road through dusty, run-down towns

where men with nothing to do sat outside their houses and watched us pass. In the distance, the separation fence, under construction, was strung out across the landscape.

After fifteen minutes or so, we came to Kdumim,* and a rough-looking bearded man with a rifle stared at our government-issued press cards, made a call and waved us through. The settlement was like every other I have seen since, small neat red-roofed houses, slightly reminiscent of Swiss chalets. The roofs are not flat like the rest of the Middle East, but pitched, as if they were expecting European levels of rainfall.

Kdumim was home to a permanent base for a support battalion, which provided combat units with food, vehicle maintenance and other services, and a holding tank for arrested Palestinians, before they were transferred to a permanent home inside the Israeli prison system.

The soldiers we were coming to see were camped temporarily on the other side of the settlement. Few people who lived there, or even those who served in the support battalion, were aware of their existence. They were paratroopers and they went where they were needed from one month to the next; they had no permanent home, but were all over the West Bank. They were

*This settlement is the home of Daniella Weiss, one of the leaders of the West Bank settler movement, who was arrested in late August 2005, when the state dismantled four West Bank settlements. In October 2004, I saw her on the night the Knesset passed the first phase of legislation to carry out the disengagement plan, screaming behind a police barrier, together with members of far-right organisations who wish to blow up the Al-Aqsa mosque so they can build the Third Temple. Her assistant was on the other side of the barrier, where the journalists were gathered, going from one to another asking if they would like to interview her. Her son, an officer in the IDF, as the disengagement was about to be implemented, asked to be removed of his command as he did not wish to carry out the orders to evacuate Gaza.

tasked with preventing suicide bombers from crossing out of Nablus and entering the towns of the coastal plain, and they did this not by establishing checkpoints on the border between the West Bank and Israel, but by ringing the city with roadblocks so that it was encircled and cut off from its hinterland, and the people from the surrounding villages who needed to go to Nablus to see a doctor or a dentist or do their shopping or carry out their ordinary business had to leave their cars miles away and either walk, white and sweating up the long hill under the still-baking October sun, or take a taxi, if they could afford one, because no private cars were allowed in or out of the city. And even ambulance drivers and doctors had to wait two or three hours while their identity card details were radioed back to the Shin Bet in Tel Aviv and join the line of other documents, waiting for a bored teenage soldier to check them against a list of names of known terrorists, because apparently Red Crescent ambulances had been used to transport terrorists or weapons or explosives. Which was denied by the Palestinians, and came to be yet another of the contested facts of the second intifada, each side insistent that they were right. But in the meantime, the doctors and ambulance drivers waited, while inside their patients grew sicker and even died.

The camp was guarded by a sleepy Ethiopian with a boom box next to him. We walked past, down a slope to a small collection of huts where the soldiers slept, and a couple of beaten-up sofas under the trees where they sat and drank coffee, and all around were these soldiers and all I could think of to say, on this first impression, was, 'Kids! They're just kids.'

We peered inside the huts. I thought I was going to see bunks with neat rolls of olive-green bedding, anally retentive army tidiness, gleaming weapons. I was expecting order, and instead there was juvenile chaos, duvet covers flung half across the floor decorated with Snoopy and space ships and Teenage Mutant Ninja

Turtles. Some soldiers had stuffed toys. Along the wall was a line of curious tails, a row of cellphone chargers plugged into their sockets, their leads dangling. There was no reveille in the camp, each soldier was to set his own cellphone alarm to wake him up. No one knew of any soldier who did not have one. In Lebanon, soldiers had used them to order pizza from a restaurant on the other side of the border.

The air was loud with several noises: the dweedly sound of cellphone ring tones downloaded from the internet permanently connecting the army of occupation with the army of the hysterically preoccupied, their mothers; plus the sound of the settlers at their evening prayers, battling it out with the call of the muezzin from a mosque nearby, drawing the Palestinians to their prayers.

The soldiers lounged around in shorts and t-shirts. One had a large marijuana leaf printed in cotton across his chest, another was tattooed across his upper arm with the face of Che Guevara, and another was reading the Hebrew translation of Anthony Beevor's account of the battle of Stalingrad. The Ethiopians gathered around a ghetto blaster listening to hip hop. It was a Vietnamised army, updated for the next century, Eminem goes camping, Eminem at Khe Sanh.

We waited an hour for the captain to arrive, and when he came I thought he must be the captain's younger brother, a short twenty-four-year-old with a round face who took us to his office, a metal freight container. He sat down at his desk behind an Israeli flag and a photograph of one of his friends who was killed in action.

I asked him where he came from, to try to situate him, from the beginning, in real life. Because he was not always a man with a uniform and a helmet and a rank, and a hundred men serving under him.

'Yavne,' he said.

'Oh,' I said, startled into recognition, 'I went to a seder in Yavne a few months ago. I can't remember the name of the family but there was a son around your age who just came out of the army. His name was Oz.' What a stupid thing to say. He's supposed to know another kid, just because he's from the same town?

'And he's working in a record store?' he asked, smiling his sweet smile, which lit up his face.

'Yes. He showed me where he cut his finger because he had to do all this gift-wrapping for pesach gifts.'

'We were in primary school together. I've known him for years.'

'His mother wants him to go to university and become a doctor.'

'I'll let you into a secret. Oz isn't going to medical school.'

So you see, my parents were right, you went to Israel and you were among family. I knew a total of five people in Yavne, and lo, Aviram knew them as well, and this helped to explain why the soldiers who appeared on the tv news at night were not the distant actors in a far-away drama of war and occupation, but your neighbour's son. And your neighbour is sitting next door, weeping as she watches her child facing a crowd of Palestinian kids armed with rocks, which could take her boy's eye out, or give him brain damage if god forbid he took off his helmet and one of those dusty stones hit him in the head.

The Hebrew name for Nablus is Shekhem, pronounced as if you're spitting out phlegm from the back of the throat, which is what most Israelis would like to do to Nablus. They call it the 'capital of terror' – from here came the bombs or bombers of the Dolphinarium nightclub in Tel Aviv in which twenty-one Russian teenagers were killed, the Park Hotel in Netanya where thirty mainly elderly people celebrating Passover were blown up, some of them Holocaust survivors, and the Sbarro pizza café in Jerusalem where fifteen died, including seven children.

Aviram began to relate his career and some of the battles he had fought in, among them the most violent and controversial of the second intifada. 'I started out in the duvduvan,' he said, 'a special unit that deals with counter-terror, where we are disguised as Arabs. I was dealing with the specific heads of terrorist organisations or with ticking bombs; I arrested the people who did the lynch of our soldiers in Ramallah – we took the guy three weeks after it happened, a nineteen-year-old. He didn't look so frightening in the middle of the night. I was involved in the arrest of Marwan Barghouti [the leader of the Tanzim, the military wing of the Fatah movement].'

After the series of suicide bombings in March 2002, culminating in the attack on the Park Hotel, the Israeli army had launched an 'incursion' into several towns on the West Bank to root out the terror cells, under the code-name Operation Defensive Shield. The refugee camp in Jenin was to one side of the town, a dense network of narrow alleys. The idea was that the soldiers would go on a search and destroy mission from house to house with a list of names and kick in the door. To the extent that the suspects were to receive any legal process, it would take place on the doorstep: 'Is this you?'

Unfortunately for the soldiers, the Palestinians knew they were coming. Whole alleys were booby-trapped and three days into the operation thirteen Israeli commandos blundered into a booby-trapped street and were blown up. Aviram saw his best friend die in front of his eyes as a wall collapsed on top of him.

The commanding officer ordered a retreat. He brought in the engineers and instead of knocking on doors, issued an order that everyone was to leave their houses and anyone who did not do so would be trapped beneath the rubble left by the bulldozers. The army now ordered a complete media blackout. This was not popular in the IDF spokesperson's department, which warned that the vacuum would be filled by rumour. They had a minibus outside their office in Jerusalem waiting to take a pool of reporters, but the commander in the field was of a higher rank than the highest ranking officer in the spokesperson's department, and after the battle for Jenin was over, there would be a reorganisation of the spokesperson's department to make sure that in the future the media could not be excluded by the commander in the field.

As predicted, the population of Jenin sent out reports that a massacre was being conducted, hundreds were dead. Emails forwarded to me at the time spoke in lurid detail of rape and murder, and in those few days the nightly news bulletins in Britain were filled with horrific second- and third-hand accounts of the piles of corpses that would be discovered when finally the press were allowed in, because this was definitely going to be a second Sabra and Shatilla, the massacre of two and a half thousand Palestinians in a Lebanese refugee camp in 1982 under the then command of the now prime minister, Ariel Sharon.

When Judah, who was covering the operation as a photographer, finally entered the camp, a week after the start of the operation, having sneaked across the dry wadis in a four-hour march, he found the centre of Jenin in ruins, a terrified and brutalised population, but no evidence of a massacre. In the end, the Palestinians declared the total number of dead was fifty-three, about half of whom were militants; others were family members who stayed inside their houses with them, or those too old or sick or disabled to be able to get out in time.

At the start of Operation Defensive Shield, Aviram was in Arafat's compound in Ramallah, and then was moved north to Jenin. 'I think I have been through every refugee camp, walking through walls,' he said. 'Jenin was the most difficult of all. There is no reason I can tell you why they were more stubborn but they fought bravely and they gave us a good fight. As a human being,

I was making the difference between the terrorists and the civilians. I don't see myself as a killer of women and children and they took advantage of that and tried to use civilians as human shields. They put bombs all over the camp, in the trees, doorways. You could see a Palestinian family surrounded by bombs. There was some strong fighting there and I guess some civilians were hit, I can't tell you by who. I know that in the eyes of Palestinians we are the occupiers and if the army was sitting in my home in Yavne, I would feel I was occupied. But suicide bombers I can't understand, it's unbelievable, after three years I still can't understand it, though I know the reasons, and they are what my company is here to stop. At the end of the day, there are people who want to kill my family, and to protect them I have to check the bags of those people and sometimes kill them.'

Every day we were with the soldiers we drove off for a few minutes to an army lookout post, near one of the roadblocks that encircled Nablus.

From the roof of the house on the edge of the village, the great bowl of the valley showed a biblical landscape, a rocky hilltop and, in the distance, the white towers of the city. Along the dusty road, Palestinian men, women and children were toiling under a hot sun, no private cars allowed to pass in or out: an old woman in a blue velvet dress, her face white and sweating; a woman holding a sick child in her arms, its eyes rolling; a water engineer trying to get to a meeting in Nablus to sign a contract, a Red Crescent ambulance with a doctor and a driver.

On the roof of the house: sandbags, camouflage netting, an Israeli flag; beyond the walls, in the garden, garbage, pizza boxes, a cardboard target of a soldier with chest sections marked. Nine months earlier the army had occupied the top floor and roof of the Turabi family's home. It was the family's bad luck that its position on the edge of the village of Tsara, overlooking all the roads from Nablus, made it an ideal watchtower. The soldiers arrived a week or so before one of the Turabi sons was due to get married and move into the new apartment his parents had built on the top floor for him and his bride. Three-quarters of a year later, there was still no wedding because there was no new apartment to move into. Concrete slabs had been raised in front of the gate; anyone who passed before their door was subject to a checkpoint, and the ones the army didn't like the look of had to put their identity documents into a slit in the side of a plastic soft-drinks bottle which was hauled up on to the roof by a piece of string for radio-checking. The soldiers told the family that they would pick up the tab for water and electricity, but though the bills had been handed over, no money had appeared yet. To add to their troubles, some people in the village called them collaborators. In the night, the family and their children were terrified; according to one of the sons, twenty-three-year-old Naeem, they heard shooting above their heads.

The mother, forbidden to pass through the locked doors of the side entrance to climb the stairs in her own house, asked me to tell her what damage the soldiers were doing up there to her son's marriage home.

When Aviram's soldiers arrived one morning to take over from another company they found the place trashed, the stairs covered with rotting garbage, floors filthy.

'They're living like pigs!' cried a sergeant with tattoos down his arm.

'But you were two hours late. Do you know what it's like to be stuck on this roof for two weeks?' the soldiers who were being relieved shouted back.

'Next time you don't wait to be woken,' their platoon commander told the arriving soldiers, 'you set the alarm on your cellphone. As for the rest of you, you're not leaving until you clean this place.'

The arriving soldiers went and lay down in bunks and fell asleep or sat around and watched videos they had rented from Blockbuster, back home when they were on weekend leave. I watched them watching the British romantic comedy *Notting Hill* and a number of episodes of *Friends*.

When you saw the soldiers lounging around on their base, they looked like teenagers in messy bedrooms, being shouted at by their wits-end parents. 'Go tidy your room! Stop eating that junk! If I catch you smoking again! For godsake what's that tattoo on your arm, who said you could get a tattoo! Get up! You're late for school!'

When you saw the same soldiers lounging around on the top floor of the Turabis' home, you had an entirely different impression; in fact, you saw the place through the eyes of the family downstairs, whose home had been invaded and desecrated by hooligans, who unlike you were protected from flying bullets by flak jackets and helmets, with nice warm coats when it was cold, who put their feet up on the furniture and scrawled graffiti on your walls and threw their filthy garbage into your garden and treated you as if you did not exist as they entered or left along the path that lay along the side of the house to the entrance you had built for your beloved son and his bride. Who never made eye contact and who knew nothing about you, for whom you were just disposable pieces of furniture to be moved about at your will.

I tried my best to understand the soldiers.

In the camp the Russians bunked with the Russians, the Ethiopians with the Ethiopians and the religious stuck together too. There was a female soldier, Aviram's secretary, and she was not allowed, by military law, to sleep with the boys, and neither was I, so at night we had to navigate a series of fences and gates and sentries to reach the support battalion where there were quite a few girls, whose lodgings were full of soft toys, murals of unicorns, and a mirror where, every morning, they gathered to tie back their hair and push at their eyelids with a mascara wand.

The boys were kids, but these were babies. You take a little girl and put her in the middle of the West Bank. Obviously she's not a little girl, she is eighteen or nineteen, but she looks much younger and it seemed to me that these minds were divided into two watertight halves, one thought soulfully of peace and peace was made up of clouds and unicorns and cuddly pets and other infantile daydreams, and the other was holed up behind barbed wire, marching to the women's jail a Palestinian her own age who had tried to stab a soldier at a roadblock because a couple of weeks earlier her brother had been killed by one of the soldiers in the paratroopers' camp.

The girls did not really know what peace meant, they did not understand that it was not merely an absence of guns and bombs. Someone would sit at a table with a paper and sign something, and it would be finished, but what was on the paper was too big for them. They didn't know.

Some of them were open; they asked questions of the prisoners they took, they tried to understand. Others relished their work. A little girl from the military police arrived wearing a tiny crop top above her jeans, her flat brown belly embellished with a belly-button piercing, dragging behind her a red suitcase on wheels like she was heading off to the airport for a vacation, and all the soldiers came out and stood at the entrance to their huts, their eyes out on stalks.

She was there to search women at the checkpoints because the Palestinian men had complained that they did not want their wives and daughters touched by an Israeli man, meddling in their honour.

There is an Arabic word that has made its way into Hebrew. A *frecha* is a slut, and the word has normally been used to describe girls of Sephardic origin, and no one with any tact would use it because it's racist. But sometimes words convey in their brutal succinctness something you could spend a paragraph explaining: Essex girl, chav, trailer trash.

Orit had grandparents from Yemen on one side and Afghanistan on the other. 'Primitive people,' she said, 'like everyone from Arab countries. Checkpoints are my job. Look, it's not fun but I have to do it. If it's not me it's someone else, and if it's not someone else it's nobody. It's a little scary but I check very good, I look at their ID, their packages and bags. I'm only nineteen but I don't think my age is important; when you hate, you hate. I hate Arabs. With everything that's going on here, how can you love them? They haven't got a heart, someone who blows up has no heart. But however much I hate them, they'll always hate me more.'

Once, in the museum that is what remains of the main camp at Auschwitz, being shown round by an insistent guide from the Polish Tourist Board, I was looking at a photograph of a very young soldier barking at a line of Jews and she asked me what I was thinking. I said that I was wondering what he was thinking.

'Nothing,' she said. 'His mind is destructed.'

I also wondered what was going on inside the heads of the smiling American soldiers, posed next to pyramids of imprisoned Iraqi flesh. Were their minds 'destructed'?

And Abdel Basset Odah, the Hamas operative from Tulkarm, who had once been a hotel worker, and who walked into the dining room of the Park Hotel in Netanya, unchallenged by the armed security guard because he did not look suspicious, and murdered himself and thirty others, mostly old ladies?

And Orit?

'I don't know Aviram any more,' said Oz a few weeks later, in an Irish pub in Rehovot where his parents sat under a giant screen, tapping their feet as Riverdance jumped up and down energetically, and Yan and Rosita and Ophir and Ilana examined the list of beers. 'Not since he came back from Jenin. Jenin changed him.'

'They won't settle,' said Ophir. Oz had been out of the army for over a year, he had done his Israeli kids' gap year, what they called the Big Trip, the travelling to Goa and Latin America and Thailand between the army and the rest of their lives. But he remained restless. When was he going to go to university, his mother kept asking.

'I was in a bar in South America,' Oz said. 'There were a bunch of us sitting around, all Israelis, all of us had done our army service, and someone said, "Each of us has a mental scratch," and we laughed, or nodded, but afterwards I thought it was true, all of us did.'

I had heard this term 'mental scratch' before. In Hebrew it is *sarut bamoach*.* The friends of one of the Russian soldiers had used it, because he was signing up for the professional army, he enjoyed taking out terrorists. 'You have to have mental scratch to do this work,' they said.

On the roof of the Turabi family's house a soldier called Udi, sitting in his underwear and a t-shirt watching the video of *Friends*, was about to leave the army in four days. He was only half a week away from finishing his three years, and he was really pissed off because it is the rule that your last two weeks of service are taken as vacation and you pack up and go and spend the next fortnight

---

*'As I said, *srita bamoach* means a mental scratch (people would normally say just "*srita*"). More often used in the form of *sarut bamoach* or just *sarut* (scratched). *Tsaleket* means a scar. I never heard it used like that, but generally it often happens that phrases are taken a step or two further, towards the extreme. So "*tsaleket*" might be an advanced stage of *srita*. At the same time, I certainly have heard my brother use the word "*charut*" (engraved) to describe an extreme case of one being *sarut* (scratched).' DB

at home, sleeping. But because of a shortage of manpower Udi had to serve every last stinking hour until he could get home to his parents in Hod HaSharon, where his father worked as a shoe salesman.

So he didn't care what he said, and didn't care about the presence of the captain from the IDF spokespersons' department, he was going to spit it out, and didn't need no interpreter either because his English was up to scratch.

'I have been sitting on this roof since last week,' he said, 'but in four days I finish with the army. I want to go home and when I get there I will stay far away from Nablus and Ramallah. If a war starts maybe I'll go and hide in the desert with the Bedouin. I never wanted not to be in the army but after three years you want to puke of the army. It gives a lot to the soldiers but enough is enough. I'm going home and I'm going to have a hot shower and sleep in my own bed. Then I'll get up and play soccer, see my girlfriend and start to live.'

I looked at the captain from the spokespersons' office, but he said nothing and so Udi kept going.

'It's obvious that a person who is not bothered about what we're doing here is lying to himself but, on the other hand, there's no other way. If I can summarise my two and a half years on the West Bank, it's going from dilemma to dilemma, one conflict to another. I'm not afraid, we're not in Vietnam, but it's not like we have someone to fight against. Our enemy is using guerrilla tactics, they're terrorists, it's not a real war. For me what is meaningful is dealing with the civilians, the Arab population, which is much more challenging. Every normal man who sees the civilians feels uncomfortable with what we're doing – and that's an understatement. That's the most amazing thing, that we're twenty and so powerful! You have to learn to control yourself and it's hard to do. The people you see in this room know how to control themselves, but there are others, children like us, and they don't.'

A few days later, I would read an article in the newspaper about a new book by Liran Ron Fuer, a former staff sergeant who served in Gaza in the mid-1990s, and who said that the army turned everyone into a violent sadist. An angry letter appeared the following week from a soldier. 'Speak for yourself,' he told him. It was Fuer's choice to be a thug.

'The army does kill children, it does, that's a fact,' Udi said. 'We can't deny it because the figures are there. Children are being killed. But every case you have to see as an individual. You can't say just because someone has been in the Israeli army he can't join some university. You don't know where he's been or what he's done, it doesn't make sense. There are a lot of people in the world who think that obeying orders is not an excuse, that sometimes we need to refuse orders, and I agree that I would refuse orders, but so far I haven't had that kind of order.

'I don't know why most of the world is against Israel right now. I see BBC, CNN, and it looks like Serbia here, like we're making a lot of war crimes. Part of the argument is probably true but you can't ignore all the bastards killing civilians who have no connection to this war. I don't think there is one of us who doesn't know someone at home who was killed or injured. We're in a very bad cycle. There are many who think that this chain of events is leading us nowhere and we have got to stop it, and then someone else will say, no, we should hit them harder, in their neighbourhoods and houses. The real point is that I'm hurting thousands of people every day, even though I don't want to. But I am not a politician, I am only the one who is saying you can pass, you can't pass.'

When we left the army base it took only twenty-five minutes to drive back to Kfar Saba. The landscape changed in an instant, as soon as we crossed the Green Line, and you could understand what the soldiers had meant when they said that they were sitting there, on the roof of the Turabis' home, trying to stop the *shahids* – the martyrs – from getting to their families in Haifa or Netanya or Rannana, it was so close.

I met Udi again. I took his cellphone number and a couple of weeks after he finished the army we met, by arrangement, on the corner of Shenkin Street in Tel Aviv and we walked down to a quiet café. On Friday mornings the teenage soldiers who had weekend passes would get on settler buses and head home or, more likely, if they were that way disposed, and many were, would make for Tel Aviv, for Shenkin, where they would meet their friends and girlfriends, drink coffee, buy some dope, make plans for the evening, go home, kiss their mothers, sleep for a few hours, eat a Friday night family meal with Sabbath candles, say nothing at all when questioned about what they had been doing for the past two weeks, then put on their party clothes and go out to a club.

A woman told me of a friend's son whom she woke one Sunday morning by touching him on the hip, and he sprang awake and tried to strangle her, because that place she had touched was where, while on duty, he kept his gun. 'And if he had the gun, she said he would have killed her,' the woman said.

Udi was standing on a windy street corner in Tel Aviv, a frail-looking boy in a large sweater and one of those hippyish Greek shoulder bags made of a piece of carpet. 'I look different without the helmet?' he said. Like two separate people, I replied. 'Well, this is the real me.'

In the café I asked him about the Udi who joined the army and the Udi who had just left. 'When you are seventeen and they start to classify you for what kind of army service you will do, most of us are still children, you don't totally understand what the army is until you get there,' he said. 'Soldiers in basic training want to fight and kill, they don't understand it will be a

trauma for life. No extreme change has occurred in me but that
is because there are two kinds of soldier, the kind who had a very
close friend who was killed in front of them, or they killed at
close range themselves, and the kind who did not. I'm glad to say
I'm in the second group, which makes me the minority.

'In the last year of the army, I had a very confusing time. I
started to question why am I guarding this settlement, why am I
not letting this sixty-year-old Palestinian through, and I think it
made me more mature and aware of who I am and who is my
neighbour. It would be very comfortable for Israel if the
Palestinians were not here and the same for them if we were not
here, but everyone knows now there are going to be two nations.'

Recently, he said, it had crossed his mind that when he travelled abroad on his post-army journey, he would be judged first as
an Israeli and an Israeli soldier. 'I will be an emissary of Israel,' he
said, 'so I will try not to get into too many arguments. If I meet
someone who has opinions about our country and if I feel he is a
reasonable person, I will be glad to talk. I know I could give him
a lot of knowledge, because I know many people are talking from
no knowledge, but if he is very extreme, I must be careful. You
cannot not think about what it means to be an Israeli, it's so
inside you. I don't think there is another nationality that is so
different and complicated. There are people in my nation I am
ashamed of, but this is my home – I have no other. I met a girl
from the Netherlands and she talked about Holland in such a
cold way, like it was just any country. When I heard that, I
realised that, with all the troubles and rough times, after all I am
still an Israeli.'

A year later, he passed through London and I took him for
coffee in Selfridges department store. He was staying at a hostel
in central London, and was planning to travel to Manchester for
a job, which would not, as it turned out, materialise. He had no
work permit. When he arrived at Heathrow he was interviewed

for four hours by immigration officers. 'But I stuck to my story,' he said, 'which was not, of course, true.' It was interesting for him, he said, to experience what it is like to be on the receiving end of the *machsom*, the checkpoint.

He had spent several months in the Galilee, building houses. He was still drifting, but he had moved a little further to the left; he wasn't sure if he was going to turn up for reserve duty.

He told me a great deal about his commander, Aviram. Judah had bumped into him at a huge peace rally in Tel Aviv, commemorating the eighth anniversary of the assassination of Yitzhak Rabin; Aviram had been on every peace rally since the prime minister had been murdered, he said.

Ophir's mother told me that Oz's mother had told her that Aviram's mother, Sophie, was a nervous wreck. She saw her crawling round the neighbourhood almost on her hands and knees because she had one son in Nablus and another son in Gaza and a daughter still at school who wanted to be a combat soldier like her brothers.

I had managed to talk Aviram into allowing me to call his mother. '*Lo lo lo lo lo lo*,' he said (the Hebrew for no) when the idea was first proposed to him. He knew what she'd say. Mothers are put on earth to embarrass their children and Sophie was no exception. 'He's a good boy,' she told me. 'He's still my baby, though he'd kill me if he heard me say it. All his soldiers on the base, they look like soldiers but they're still babies, they need someone to hug them. Two weeks ago he was sick and I wasn't there to be able to make him soup. How do you think that makes me feel?

'Everything he does I'm proud of, but I'm sure that it has a big effect,' she continued. 'Jenin was something very meaningful for his life. He wasn't the same Aviram as I knew before, and it was the same with my husband when he came back from Lebanon. But we talk about it a lot, we are a very open family, and it's important that he hears what we have to say. That out of all this death the meaning of life will be more important to him. We want him to be a human being who can still see the eyes of the other.'

One night Aviram came into the hut where he slept and found Judah showing the reservist from the IDF spokespersons' office a slide show on his laptop of the photographs he had taken in Jenin. You could not smell in those dusty images the stench of rotting flesh, of the people and animals trapped underground in the ruins of the demolished buildings, said Aviram.

A child stands in the centre of the apocalypse, biting her nails, with a demented expression in her eyes; women wander through a landscape of death and loss, walls that Aviram himself had broken, houses he had destroyed or entered at gunpoint. I watched his face, lit up by the screen, as the images clicked away in front of him. 'Sad pictures,' he said quietly, then, with almost no pause, 'did you know three of our soldiers were killed in an ambush today? Young boys.'

In Selfridges, Udi tried to explain to me about minds that are divided, how you live with the part of you that shoots terrorists in cold blood and kills civilians, and blows up houses with people inside them, by making a space inside your head that is against the occupation and is waiting for the man to come who will sit down with the paper and write the things that will end it. Aviram's parents wanted their son to be a *mensch*, not a war criminal. Perhaps all soldiers, in all wars, moral or immoral, legal or illegal, on whatever side you fight on, bury something in an iron box beneath their chests.

Aviram had under his command Yonatan, one of the army's top snipers, a slight, good-looking dark boy with beautifully shaped sideburns and his combat pants worn halfway down his hips like he was a member of an LA street gang. 'You have to understand that this is a war,' Yonatan had said to me. 'There is a moral imperative to every operation. I have got no feeling or conscience about anyone I have killed; there is a reason and it's done to standard procedures. And when I finish in the army I will go to New Zealand and Australia, to try to find another reality.'

In Selfridges, among the well-heeled shoppers, I knew that I had understood very little about the soldiers when I was amongst them. I didn't understand that they left the army and returned to civilian life, each with their *sarut bamoach*. 'There was someone I knew in school who did his army service and he came back, he got married, had kids, everything was normal, then one day when he was thirty, he shot his wife, his kids and himself,' Udi had said.

You saw the effect of the *sarut bamoach* in the road rage, the domestic violence, the short-fuse temper of people standing in line in the supermarket.

And you had to wonder about the generation of boys and girls who were the soldiers of the second intifada, about what of their experience they would take forward into the future. It was only realistic to wonder if they were going to become a lost generation, a Vietnam generation; if, in ten years' time, there would be a surge in suicides, heroin addiction, alcoholism, divorce, child abuse and men hitting women, thrashing dogs, a sudden yen for taking up bloodsports like shooting birds and other animals.

But mostly, you just saw them walking round, rattling a bit, like shells that have had their explosives expended and are now just corroded metal. Except, as I kept insisting, they are not metalmen, but flesh and blood. I wrote in the *Guardian* that when I had seen Udi on the windy street in Tel Aviv, he looked so young and frail that I wanted to make of myself a human shield, to protect him against all the hate and demonisation he was going to encounter when he left the army and travelled abroad, and a pair of outraged readers wrote a letter, which was published, saying that if I wanted to do something useful, I could go to Palestine and make myself a human shield for the children that Udi and his friends were killing on a daily basis.

And so it went on, the fight to the death over who it was, in this conflict, that actually was a human being, and who were the real barbarians: the war of the photographs, where even poetry clamorously demands its right to take sides.

Gush Katif

The day of the big *balagan*, when I tripped and fell into the bath and nearly drowned, I had come home empty-handed from a trip to the Carmel Market, across the road from Shenkin Street, which is my favourite place in Israel. It was here, five years earlier, that I had first seen a Jewish hooker and her Jewish pimp, a Jewish beggar and a Jewish drug dealer, and knew that the dream of the first prime minister, David ben Gurion, who said that Israel would be a normal country when the first Jewish policeman arrested the first Jewish prostitute, had been fulfilled. But I knew that already because a small item in the *Jerusalem Post* on the items under discussion in the Knesset health subcommittee had caught my eye. Coolly, it stated that a seventy-five-year-old Tel Aviv prostitute with full-blown Aids had been found a place in an old people's home in Tiberias. I have always wanted to write a short story about the *alter kackers* in the old-age home smoothing back their thin strands of hair and rubbing one decrepit shoe against a trouser leg, awaiting the arrival of the hottie from the big city, but 'blow jobs only, lady, I don't want no diseases.'

What a crowd, what a rush, what a press of humanity in that market, the crying, the singing, the calling out of the stallholders: a lot of them were Arabs from Jaffa, and a lot of them were sour angry Likudniks with posters of Arik Sharon pasted on the wall behind them, and others had those pictures propped up against the fruit and veg of Sephardi rabbis with long beards and strange paraphernalia. And you just took this turn, *here*, and you were in a maze of sun-bleached Yemenite streets, where old people sat smoking really cheap cigarettes and drinking very strong coffee and gabbing and they looked up at me and thought, 'Tourist.'

But I didn't get into the market, to rifle through oriental CDs and inhale the sharp, black, oily odour of vats of olives, or step by mistake on a rotting orange, because just as I was about to enter, my cellphone rang and it was Jonathan, who is the only Israeli I know who can tell me what is really going on inside the Right, inside the very heart of the Likud party. So instead of saying I'd call him back, I asked him what the deputy prime minister Ehud Olmert had meant a few days ago when, in an interview in *Ha'aretz*, he had spoken of taking some kind of unilateral steps to get out of Gaza and four small West Bank settlements, and what did Ariel Sharon think?

I went and sat down on a concrete bench near the man who sold lottery tickets and for forty minutes listened and peppered Jonathan with questions. He was exceptionally bright, right wing but not religious, and his mind ranged around the region, looking at the long- and short-term consequences of this or that government policy. The Olmert interview, he told me, was what they call in politics a trial balloon – let's see how it goes down with the public – but the idea was all Sharon's own. The government had come to the conclusion that Yasser Arafat was never going to sit down at a table and sign a peace deal with Israel, he was an old-style revolutionary in the mould of Fidel Castro, he wanted total victory, a million *shahids* marching on Jerusalem, not some weaselly legalistic bullshit giving away the rights of his people which, anyway, weren't his to give. He was directly funding terror, the government said, and you just had to ignore him, pretend he wasn't there, rotting in the Muqata, the presidential compound in Ramallah, free to leave, but with no guarantees that he would be able to return.

So one day the government had woken up and realised that within a generation there would be a majority of Palestinians between the river Jordan and the Mediterranean sea; and soon the call would come for a single state, like in South Africa the Jews would be a minority, back where they had started. The Zionist dream, from the very beginning, was to find the one place in the world where they would be free to determine their own fate, make their own laws, defend themselves, without being beholden to the goodwill of others. For Israel to survive as a Jewish state, one which existed to be a national home for the Jewish people, it had to redefine its borders. It was going to have to cut loose some of the occupied territories, and first on the list was Gaza, which no Israeli loved and where no Israeli ever went. The only question, Jonathan said, is whether the Americans will let us.

Ten months later, when the government was about to vote to dismantle the Gaza settlements, Judah and I went there and spent five days living among the settlers. It was not so difficult a place to enter as the West Bank. We rolled south through peaceful fields green and yellow in the October sunshine. We drove parallel with

most of the Gaza Strip, until we turned west and passed a single
bored soldier on a roadblock and entered the moon.

Churned-up sand, tank tracks, barbed wire. Nothing is
allowed to grow on this buffer zone between the two lands.

We drive on, along a two-lane highway, behind SUVs and
other expensive vehicles. Parallel to it is a single track along
which Palestinian schoolchildren in white scarves walk smartly,
and men carry things on donkeys and very old trucks, and behind
them is Al-Mawasi, a Palestinian and Bedouin shanty town of
dilapidated shacks, and beyond that I glimpse the sea, the same
sea I watched from the balcony on the first apartment on
Ruppin, which is indifferent to everything but its own fishy,
salty, sea-sailed purpose. The people of Al-Mawasi were penned
in, between the road they couldn't drive along and the shore, a
narrow ghetto cut off from the rest of Gaza and the rest of the
world. When they closed off Al-Mawasi at the beginning of the
intifada, all the residents were registered and given personal
numbers without which they could neither leave nor enter, like
branded cattle. There is no cemetery in Al-Mawasi. When a
woman died, her husband tried to take her body in a car across
the checkpoint but was told the vehicle could not go through
and ended up carrying her in his arms. For five months at the
height of the intifada, fishermen were forbidden to go to sea. If
they could fish, the catch spoiled in the heat while it waited at
checkpoints. Long lines of cars form to drive produce out of the
town for sale. Stuck behind a van full of fruit, I watched a soldier
help himself. The driver held out his arms and gestured at us,
helplessly. It was a very unpleasant sight for me, watching this
swaggering Jewish thief who thinks he is entitled, as a *droit de
seigneur*, to other people's hard-earned property. He reminded
me of the Cossacks.

When we come to the gates of Neve Dekalim, the adminis-
trative and shopping capital of Gush Katif, the southern bloc of

Gaza settlements, the security gets far more ferocious. Soldiers pull us over and make phone calls and check our documents, and only after a lot of suspicious looks and questions are we allowed to enter the dream world of middle America, the placid lawns and quiet public square fringed with palm trees that exists, as a kind of reverse ghetto, behind barbed wire, fed by the life-support system of the army, without which, in a matter of hours, it would be overrun by the thousands of angry, impoverished people who lie in wait in the Khan Younis refugee camp, a few metres away behind a high wall at the back.

The settlers go about their business, which is agriculture. They grow all kinds of things in the hothouses they have built by the sea: organic tomatoes, pot plants, herbs that are free of bugs and thus suitable for the ultra kosher market. Some Palestinians cross the checkpoints to work in the greenhouses, but no longer very many since the start of the intifada, and they have been replaced by foreign labourers from Thailand and the Philippines who are really good at growing flowers, because here in Gaza much of the world's lily production is raised, and the bouquets that decorated the various shrines to Princess Diana in the days after her death grew in this earth, were picked by these hands.

The square has a large town hall and, to the side, various small shops and cafés and a supermarket. Settlers come from across the Gush, from the tiny villages, some housing only twenty families, to shop and go to the post office to do various paperwork business. They don't look anything like the Jews of West Jerusalem, with black hats, black beards. They don't look anything like the hilltop youth of the remoter reaches of the West Bank, those *meshuggayim* dressed like hippies in tie-dye shirts with long hair and long *peyas* (sidelocks), who, in a kind of ecstatic trance, dance on the hilltops and then run out and make a pogrom against the Palestinians and poison their olive trees and do all sorts of unpleasant vicious mischief, thumbing their noses at the army, or even attacking them and stealing their weapons.

There are no hilltop youth in Gaza because there aren't any hills. The topography is undulating and duney, but the bare out-crops of the Judean desert are not here. These are law-abiding individuals, religious, but not Hassids. They don't come from Poland or Brooklyn; most of them are from Tunisia or Morocco, or originally from there via France, the Jewish *pieds noir* of post-colonial North Africa. The women have dark hair and dark eyes and they wear nice, round-brimmed hats to cover their hair, and to the extent that you can do a lot with the restrictions of a modest dress code, they are proud of their appearance and even quite fashionable. In fact, it's explained to me how settler dress has its changing trends, from one season to the next. A young girl who runs the stationery shop, where I go to buy a handful of Bic pens, is in tight pink pants and a tight pink top and I want to know how this could possibly be a fulfilment of the Orthodox dress code, but she says, 'Look at my arms. The sleeves come just below the elbow.' So? What's so sexy about the elbow? She crooks it and the flesh of her arms folds around a cleft. 'It's sup-posed to remind them of something,' she says, her eyes sparkling with mischief. Where's your hat? I say. 'I don't need to wear one yet, I'm not married.' When will you get married? 'When my boyfriend gets out of the army.' How long have you known him? 'We were in Bnei Akiva together, the religious youth group.'

In a little office in the admin building, Eran Sternberg is hunched over the tv. He has small eyes in a potato face, his *kippah* pinned to his head, beige combat pants, boots. *Shtarker* is written all over him. He's watching a video of yesterday's rally against disengagement, a week before the Knesset will vote on the matter. He's smiling. Never never never never.

I sat down with my notebook. Neve Dekalim was swarming with journalists, the first crucial Knesset vote was taking place in a few days. Queues of reporters, photographers and tv crews from across the world stood in line outside Eran's office. Nothing happened without his say-so, he was the chosen head of the Struggle Committee. If you wanted to speak to anyone, you had to go through him; if you stopped anyone and asked them a question, they said, 'Does Eran know about you?' Eran's assistant, Debbie Rosen, had an approved list of interviewees. Everyone wanted to talk to English speakers and she was in charge of sending them to the handful of Americans and one British family who lived in Gush Katif.

'So, Eran,' I asked, 'what do you think Sharon is up to? Why do you think he's doing this to you?' For Ariel Sharon was said to be the father of the settlement movement. Like Moses he pointed to the promised land and said, go hence and multiply, in Gaza, Hebron, Judea and Samaria. Plant and populate. Or rather, when he was minister of housing, he built houses and gave people low mortgages and tax breaks.

'Sharon is surrounded by snakes and vipers,' Eran said. 'He knows very well that the elitists, the left, are the ones who write the history books and make the legal decisions. He presents it as a done deal but he hasn't succeeded yet in moving one caravan. He knows the strength of the resistance and that there is total opposition in the army. There's a psychological war to hope we'll evict ourselves by our own free will. [Dov] Weissglass and the other snakes have persuaded him. But it won't happen; 4589 mortar shells have fallen on Gush Katif and only one person has been killed. I have an update every few hours here on my laptop. These are the miracles we have seen, so how can I believe that God means to evict us?'

I have met some colourful characters in my life, but none to compare with the New Yorkers Moishe and Rachel Saperstein. We were invited to breakfast; we had an introduction from a guy in Jerusalem whom Judah had known since the 1960s, back in America, so we sat down in their pleasant house and a lavish spread of food was laid out before us and Moishe sat down too, his empty sleeve hanging against his shirt where his arm was blown off in a terrorist attack as he was driving the settler-only road, and up on his face an eye was missing because of another explosion. The man was in bits. He had on display a rocket, which looked like something you make in metal shop at trade school, with Arabic letters on it spelling out Al-Quds – Jerusalem. It had landed in his garden.

Wow, could they talk. Moishe was like a cross between Jackie Mason and Moishe Dayan. You do not expect someone with whom you so profoundly disagree, someone you think is really wrong, really dangerous, who has a head full of horrible ideas, to make you laugh so much you're wiping the tears from your face.

And not only that, breakfast was delicious, but when it became apparent that we were on the wrong side, the *other* side, we were the hated left, the peaceniks, the Arab-lovers, the terrorist-appeasers, the smile fell off Rachel's face, and she snatched away my plate while I was in mid-mouthful.

'I'm at war,' Moishe said, refilling the coffee machine.

'Who are you at war with?' Judah shouted across the kitchen at him.

'You name it. With the Arabs, with the Jews who support the Arabs, with my countrymen who refuse army service.'

I tried to ask a question, one I knew he wouldn't like. I tried to cushion it – I had been eating the man's food. 'Moishe, I know you won't like this question, but I have to ask it, it's my job . . .'

'So you're just doing your job. Like Eichmann.'

'Listen,' I said, having had enough of this nonsense, 'if my father was alive now to hear you compare his daughter to Eichmann, he'd come down here and tear your other arm off.'

Moishe stopped, and looked at me. He saw it now, how things were. I was a Jewish daughter and he was a Jewish father, and now I was his daughter, and he knew, and I knew what that meant. Things had moved to another level, and the wisecracks stopped and he got serious.

'If you sit down and look at the position of Israel, realistically you'd pack up and leave,' he said. 'Our situation is hopeless. In the Negev there is a Bedouin majority. In the north, if you take out Haifa, there are more Muslims than Jews. If you don't believe that it's the Jewish destiny to be here, then you're a fool to hang around.

'Mr Sharon has no belief in Jewish destiny. He's simply buying time. The government will buy several months after they give up Gush Katif, then they'll have to give up something else, then they'll give up everything. If someone could show me how my leaving here would benefit Israel I would swallow my bile and leave, but nobody has made the argument. As a believer, I believe that all will be well in the end, but I have no idea what God is planning. Our chances of surviving Sharon are two in five, there is no real strong opposition to him. I can't see any way out. So Sharon goes and we get Netanyahu. So what? He has a spaghetti spine. I don't see any relief from him.'

I asked them what would happen when the time came. They would go on the roof and make their stand, they said, then they would leave quietly. Would they shoot?

'God forbid we would kill a soldier,' Rachel said, looking at me in disbelief that I would suggest such a thing. 'He's someone's kid, he's a Jewish boy, who am I to attack him?'

Months later, it occurred to me that some of the soldiers who would be coming to take them from their home would be Druze and Bedouin, and whether that might be a different matter, when it came to asking yourself who you could and could not shoot back at.

*

A two-storey house set in a cul-de-sac, surrounded by palm trees and trees bearing huge flowers and luscious, exotic fruits.

Up the steps, a two-bedroom holiday apartment, from the time when religious Jews would come to spend their vacation at the devout seaside holiday resorts of Gush Katif. No Jews are coming from Israel now, just journalists and writers and cameramen, to whom Ronni Bakshi has to rent the place out to supplement his income from driving the Magon David Adom ambulance, which is parked outside the house.

At night the wide balcony is rocked by the thud of the mortars and the rockets. It goes on for hours. They are firing from Khan Younis. Gunshot is heard, the Israeli soldiers firing across the wall into the town. A great firefight breaks out, helicopter gunships hovering overhead, making their giant noise, tank shells banging, a noise that makes your head want to break, and your heart is bursting in terror against your chest. And Ronni's five kids in the flat below turn over in their sleep, because this is normal and they know that they are warriors in the fight for the land.

The whole family was always moving, and always being moved on. Ronni's father came from Iraq. Fleeing with his nine brothers in 1948 to Iran, they invested their money in carpets but were cheated by an Iranian partner. They arrived in Israel with nothing. When Israel conquered the Sinai from the Egyptians in 1967, he moved from Jerusalem to Yamit. When, after the 1978 peace treaty, Israel handed the Sinai back, Yamit was the lone settlement that clung on to the death, determined to repel the evacuation. Ronni was an eighteen-year-old student at the *yeshiva* [religious school] who had come back home to Yamit to stand by his mother and father, to thwart the army dragging them from their homes. He saw his father arrested, his mother in the house crying. Somewhere around there, as yet unmet, was his future wife. Her father emigrated to Israel from Syria. He was one of the ideologues who went to Yamit six months before the evacuation to be part of the showdown with the army.

'The word disengagement is symptomatic of people who have no roots,' Ronni said, 'who have no connection to the land, and this is an absurd notion in the Middle East where land is what defines you.' He couldn't understand the mentality of a government that would drive people from their homes, which did not understand the sweat and struggle it took to build a community. In the basement of the community centre I had found a Russian clarinet player, a man who had once been a member of the Leningrad Philharmonic, teaching children to play. The boy would be flung back across the Green Line in one direction, the clarinet player in another, and all the little nerve endings of communal networks would die.

I felt some sympathy for Ronni. He had his beliefs, which were not mine, but it's always agony to see something you have built destroyed. The emotions aren't fake.

He could walk a few metres away, I suggested, behind the wall at Khan Younis, to the refugee camp, and meet people who have the exact same experience. In 1948 they had fled or been driven from their homes. They remember houses that had been in their families for generations. Twenty years is a long time, but behind the wall are people who hold keys to houses built in the era of Napoleon. Do you understand their agony, too?

'That's a good question,' he said, not evading it, but then we got badly lost in a biblical argument about the ownership of the land, and arguments about who had started the 1948 war.

What are you going to do when the soldiers come? How will you protect your children?

'I want them to go through the trauma,' he said. 'I want them to experience it so afterwards they know how to relate to their country, not to serve in its army. The difference between here and Yamit is that Yamit did not have the history of sacrifice and tragedy that this community has. People have fought and died and been murdered here, which makes the people much more bitter about being disposed of. The government is waging psychological war against us, but we live in an environment of danger, we will not be intimidated.'

I asked him if he would pick up a gun and shoot if the army came to drag him from his home.

'I try not to think about that,' he said. 'It's not simple. There's no historic precedent, which is why it's so hard to get my head round it. In Yamit I hadn't built or grown anything, yet still we sat and cried.'

No one was leaving, no one would budge an inch. The disengagement plan would fail, there would be a referendum and the public would throw it out, hundreds of thousands of people would come and join the mass protests, they would shut the country down, there was total solidarity. (Apart from one lone individualist, Meir Rosenstein, who ran an electrical store but it was being boycotted, his son bullied and ostracised at school, and nobody paid him any attention, apart from all the reporters who interviewed him in droves.)

In every small town in America there is a drugstore and behind the counter, dishing out the burgers and home fries, is a big girl with big tits and a big heart and a big mouth. You have to have a type like this to keep the customers in line, someone sociable and yappy and flirtatious, so in Neve Dekalim there was Miriam, who was twenty-four and still not married and on the lookout for a husband among the many soldiers who dropped in in their army trucks for ice cream and coffee or a sandwich. Except they were just kids, eighteen or nineteen, too young, so where was she ever going to find a guy?

Miriam hears and sees everything. She has her own point of view.

'Why is Sharon doing this? Somebody that fat can't be all there mentally,' she said. 'Somebody that fat spends all his time thinking about food and so he doesn't have time to think about the real problems. But my feeling is that most of the people here are prepared to take the money and run. There is an incredible amount of hypocrisy. When the media come they're taken round to the hardliners, but I know the people and what they say in the café. They're fed up and all the talk is of leaving. This business of the tunnels is driving people crazy, the mortars, the rockets, they're not just for television. The media portrays us as a bunch of ignorant hooligans living on a hilltop by the sea but we're just the same as anyone else.

'I didn't vote in the last election because I didn't believe in any of the candidates, I believe in God. If anyone knocks on my door to pull me out, I'm not going to put up a fight. I still live with my parents, my father is a farmer, so we want to go to a *moshav* [an agricultural village] outside one of the big cities in Israel. I'm not a spoiled child, what's good for my parents is good for me. I just want to meet someone and get married.'

Sometimes her brother would pull up in his Alfa Romeo; it was his café. He lived on the beach in the most bizarre settlement in the whole of the occupied territories, a former hotel where a bunch of single guys had moved in and surfed and had barbecues and brought back their girlfriends. I spoke to one of them, wandering across the sand with a book. It was a novel by José Saramago, the Portuguese Nobel Prize-winning novelist who had returned from Gaza and pronounced it no different from Auschwitz. I raised this with him. Saramago was misunderstood, he said, and anyway, he could forgive him because he was such a great writer. The hotel was surrounded by guard towers and barbed wire, like a holiday camp that had modelled itself on a German POW facility. At the entrance dogs howled and bared their teeth; in one direction was Rafah, in the other was Gaza

City. The nine single men managed to live a very nice life, on the beach. They could not see why it shouldn't continue.* They weren't religious, they didn't think God had granted them these few metres of shoreline; they didn't hate the Palestinians. They couldn't see why they couldn't stay where they were, at peace with their neighbours. In a single state? I asked. No! they replied, shocked. So they would become Palestinians, apply for citizenship? They laughed, no, obviously not. So they would continue to be Israelis and the Palestinians would be citizens of where, what country?

And this was the brick wall I always drove into. They didn't know. They had no answer.

They knew they were in a situation, and that they had a problem, but they couldn't see that the problem was them, and the solution to the problem was them, too.

Late at night. The sky blazing with shellfire and mortar rounds, the settlement tannoy shouting get indoors get indoors get indoors, and the coffee shop is still open and on the bench outside the teenagers are sitting, because where there is a small town with a coffee shop there are bored teenagers who have nothing to do, because in small-town life there isn't anything to do, except sit in the drugstore and watch MTV on the tv screen that's in the window, so this is it, in the middle of the firefight, which is taking place because the Israeli army has just assassinated the engineer of the Qassam rockets in Khan Younis and the factions are retaliating, trying to throw everything they have

---

*Two months before the disengagement, the young men were driven out of the hotel by several hundred fanatics from far-right West Bank settler communities armed with automatic weapons, who had entered the Gush and set up on the beach in order to have a Masada-style shootout with the army. Ophir had tried to enter the beach area with a uniformed reservist but they were repelled. The West Bank extremists were later themselves driven out by the army.

into Neve Dekalim, and the army is throwing everything they have, which is a great deal more, back at them. And the kids are still sitting there, absorbed and absent from this scene, checking out how the people on the screen are dressed and what their hair is all about, right now. Like the nucleus inside the atom inside the molecule, that is of itself and nothing else, they are their own world.

The boys have long ponytails and baggy shorts and t-shirts with slogans on them, and earrings and tattoos; the girls wear teeny-weeny skirts and their flat brown bellies are pierced with rings. When they walk in, the Orthodox girls giggle and turn red.

In every small town, as well as a coffee shop and a Miriam, there are the dangerous kids, the kids from the wrong side of the tracks, the outlaws. The ones who have a leather jacket and whose parents don't nag and *nudge* and *kvetch* at them to get on with their homework or they'll never get to be a Harvard MBA. Like the Fonz in *Happy Days*.

Ask them about the disengagement plan. 'Wha?' Ask them about the battle going on above their heads. 'Wha?'

They're the children of the secular settlers, the ones whose mothers and fathers came to Gaza because they were living in arsehole-of-the-universe places like Bat Yam, in a cramped apartment whose window overlooked someone else's cramped apartment, with its stinks and raised voices.

Ariel Sharon had offered them a cheap house to buy or rent, right by the sea, and the opportunity for good jobs in agriculture or construction, and they wanted more for themselves and their families – fresh air, small-town life, low crime rates, good schools, no bad influences, no drug dealers, plenty of work – so they took the offer. The land had been conquered fair and square in 1967, winner keeps all. And they would be pioneers, just as the early Zionist pioneers had built something from nothing. These nobodies, these ordinary people no one ever paid much attention to, were going to be heroes of the settlement movement, not because they ever opened a Bible and read about how Samson had gone to Gaza to *shtup shiksas* and then got stuck in a Philistine jail, or because of any promise God had made to Moses, but because they were to be the brave and lonely outposts against the enemy, the Arab millions who if they had half a chance would drive them, as threatened, into the sea.

The secular settlements of Gush Katif lay along the road, small satellites with no infrastructure of their own, just the same barbed-wire fence, the same suspicious soldier on guard, but leaving Neve Dekalim and its villas, the communities seemed more desolate and windswept. The sand came up to the very doors of the houses. A few metres away lay the sea, inaccessible; since the start of the intifada it had been too dangerous to walk down there.

At Peat Sadeh a row of one-storey houses lay empty. 'We built them, and no one came.' The roofs were already losing their tiles and seabirds used them to deposit their guano.

A Bedouin from Al-Mawasi was working on the road. He had been employed by the Gush Katif council for more than twenty years. He was very dark-skinned, working all day in the sun.

'Is the disengagement going to happen?' I asked him.

'Ariel Sharon gets what Ariel Sharon wants,' he said.

'What about those houses, do you think you're going to live in them one day?'

'You think they're going to give a road-mender like me one of these places? The party officials from Ramallah are going to take them as their summer villas.'

I have been trying to discover what the name Peat Sadeh means. Literally, it is a corner of a field, and this could be taken as a metaphor, Judah suggested, 'a little piece of heaven'. The residents were all secular. A *mikvah*, the ritual bath-house for Orthodox women, lay unused at the edge of the village. Sand crept up on everything. You could see along the shore a line of large villas, holiday homes of rich Palestinians. We drove the car too far into the dunes and had to find someone with a truck to haul us out. A man in his forties with a bushy ponytail arrived driving a four-by-four; his name was Doron and he was head of Peat Sadeh security.

One time, several years before, Vicky Sabaj's Argentinian husband, an electrician by trade, came back from his reserve duty and told his wife, 'I've seen a place. It's the place you have been dreaming of all your life. Come with me and take a look at it.'

She had been born in Vienna after the war. She wasn't a Zionist until 1967 when Israel won the Six Day War and Leonard Bernstein came to her city to conduct a concert, and when the orchestra played 'Hatikva', the Israeli national anthem, she stood and sang and knew she was finished with Austria. She left at once to come to Israel, to be part of the socialist experiment of kibbutz life, but after a couple of years she knew that she would always be an incomer there; she wanted to be like the first pioneers, a founder of something, of a new community.

She wandered across the world and wound up in Mozambique at the time of independence. 'Most people who knew me before would have thought that this was the last place I would go,' she said, sitting in her house. Her husband, who had been on night-shift, woke up and came into the kitchen in his jeans, rubbing his eyes. 'Well, you can see he's younger than me. He came to my house one day to fix something and we sat and talked and talked and he never left. When I was in Mozambique I had no sympathy with the Portuguese settlers who had been sitting on the backs of the Africans for five hundred years. Everyone was frantic because the Frelimo were coming. I walked out on the street and I saw this little black guy with a Kalashnikov and a guitar, he was cute, really cute. Everyone was scared, but the Frelimo had the good grass and the spoilt settler kids would meet them on the street corners to smoke grass with them. The Frelimo were less bitter and less hostile than the Palestinians. The Palestinian police came here after Oslo and they were not local and they repressed their own and a lot of Palestinians I know were scared shitless.

'I had a child with a Portuguese army officer and I went with him to Portugal, but it didn't work out, so I came back to Israel. To join the settlements you have to take psychometric tests and be interviewed by the Jewish Agency. This guy says to me, you went all over the world, how do you think you are going to sit in a little place like that? I said, the rest of the world is only scenery.

'I didn't come here as an ideologue, but the ideology grows on you, it comes from the place. I think every place you live colours how you think; people make places, but places also make people. And obviously I'm not getting rich on the backs of the Arabs – look around you, I own nothing. This house is rented from the government.

'I never trusted Sharon, I always thought he was unpredictable. I don't trust anyone now. I used to run a restaurant on the beach. I was twelve hours a day with an Arab worker and I said that if there was a terrorist attack I was sure he would protect me, but today there has been too much blood. Something has broken, there is too much distrust. I'm not running around shouting death to the Arabs, but when they killed my friend's husband I stopped wanting to know.'*

I told her I thought that the Gush Katif settlers seemed different to the West Bank settlers. 'That's true,' she said. 'Revolutionaries always come from the hills, never from the beach. Castro came from the hills, not the coast.'

*The village had a widow, a woman in jeans, lately with a gun on her hip at all times, whose husband was shot at point-blank range by one of his Palestinian workers in the hothouses.

Her fifteen-year-old son Yochana came home. I recognised him immediately, he was one of the kids sitting outside the coffee shop. He had lived in that house since he was two years old. His life was the beach and his dogs. He had to be bussed over the Green Line twenty kilometres, because that was the nearest secular school. They would hitchhike to Israel to go to a club.

'These are the dangerous boys,' Vicky said. 'When my big boy was going out with a religious girl, her father put up a big fight. He's an officer now and they still won't give him the time of day. But according to what my son tells me, those religious girls are having sex, no matter how they're dressed.'

I could have talked to Vicky for hours; in fact, I did talk to her for hours. An idea was creeping up on me, something Moishe Saperstein had said when I asked him how he could live like this.

'We're on the edge of anxiety all the time, but how else do you know you're alive?' he had said.

Vicky did not want to leave her house; she was right behind the Struggle Committee. A secret meeting had just taken place between some of the residents of Peat Sadeh and the Disengagement Authority, a negotiation to see if they could be moved, as a community, across the Green Line instead of being dispersed. Despite Eran's loud cries of solidarity, people were secretly poring over real estate brochures. But she was not part of that group, which surprised me because I assumed she was a pragmatist, but of course this was a partial misreading – she was a hippie, a dreamer. She said that when the army finally came, she would be long gone, she was not someone who believed in lost causes. But where would she go? 'Back to the mainland, with everyone else,' she said, 'back to being asleep.'

For to live in Gush Katif was not only to live on an island, but also to be part of an heroic adventure. It was to wake up in the morning and to know that your life had purpose and meaning, that you were fulfilling something, a deeper destiny. Though some drove expensive SUVs and had swimming pools, the people of Gush Katif were not really materialists. If this had motivated them, they would be living in Herzlyia, the slick high-tech town on the coast above Tel Aviv. The shallowness of Israeli society sickened them. Here, in the centre of Gaza, in the heart of the enemy's land, you knew you were someone exceptional. There is a hunger to live a life of meaning, intense longings for coherence, for a communal existence endowed with morality and purpose, to care and feel and know that you are for something, not aimless, not pushed around. A 'hook on the soul'. Passion.

'To know that radiance, to be lit from within, and then to lose it; to be thrown back, away from its light and heat; to know thereafter the ordinary greyness of life ...' The writer Vivian Gornick, speaking of the American members of the Communist Party, into which she was born: Jews who came to America and found there an ideology which made them bigger, better, more moral and more thinking than the great mass of humanity that was trampled on by capitalism.

It seems perverse to compare the Jewish settlers of Gush Katif with the principled communists of 1930s New York, the Bronx and Brooklyn, who had a universal vision of equality and justice. But ideas do not exist independently from the people who hold them, ideas can only be transmitted and put into practice by human flesh and blood. It is not enough to win the argument intellectually; debate is insufficient to persuade someone to sign up to a cause.

The settlers of Gush Katif had come originally to Gaza to make a better life for their families. But what they found there was a sense of being part of the great struggle of the Jewish people for survival; they saw themselves as links in a chain that stretched back across the millennia, to the covenant God made with Moses and all that happened in between. They lived a dream of elevating yourself beyond suffering. To be a settler in Gaza was not just a right, but also a duty: a duty to an idea of redemption and endurance and courage.

That's how they saw it, that's how they felt.

At the back of Neve Dekalim there was an industrial zone, a series of small factories bottling fruit juices and binding stationery. A monstrous high concrete wall in front of which tanks were parked, like children's toys jumbled across the floor. Behind the wall lay Khan Younis. I could not go there. Between the two towns there was only a few metres, you could walk from one to the other, and a line of Palestinians stood waiting at the checkpoint that would admit them to the factories – that is, those very few who were trusted enough, trusted even more than the Thai workers, to enter that sealed-off area, a no-man's land between California and the Third World.

I didn't walk across, not because I was incurious or lazy, but because the separation between the two was so complete that we would have had to drive north two hours to Jerusalem, hire a car with Palestinian licence plates, hire a translator and a fixer, then enter from a completely different checkpoint, one which did not abut onto a settlement.

And if I had been in Khan Younis it would have been the same had I wanted to enter Neve Dekalim: leave the Gaza Strip, drive back to Jerusalem, drop off the car with the Palestinian plates, pick up a car with Israeli plates and turn round and go back where you had come from.

The two worlds were watertight compartments. They were almost invisible to each other. The Palestinians saw the settlers drive in their fancy cars along their nice roads, and saw the red roofs of their houses in the distance. The settlers saw the Palestinians on foot, waiting to cross the checkpoints. Out of the corner of their eyes they thought they saw armed shadows on the road.

The flame of the settlers' belief in what they did cast a very small halo of light on the world that surrounded them. They did not see, did not want to see, would not see, would make damned sure it was *impossible* to see the suffering that their presence caused on the people who lived so close like a knife to their necks.

Over and over again they told me that they would never leave; God would not permit it, a miracle would save them.

But no miracle from God had saved the Jews in the Holocaust, I pointed out, and if God remained silent in the worst catastrophe in the whole of Jewish history, why should he speak now?

The settlers of Gush Katif said that they were there because God wanted them to be there, and because they had lived a righteous life, had walked in the ways of the Lord and obeyed his commandments, unlike the secular heathens of Tel Aviv. God would protect his people and make sure that no harm came to them. The children of Israel had wandered for forty years in the wilderness, and while they did, God made them a covenant. He stretched out his hand and showed them the land he was giving to them in exchange for obedience to the great truth of Judaism, its first commandment: 'I am the Lord thy God and thou shalt have no other God before me.'

Their return was the fulfilment of that historic destiny, therefore it was simply impossible for the government of Israel to remove them, because to do so would be for man to set himself up over God.

At midnight on Sunday 15 August 2005, the settlers lost their battle with the state. The army closed off the border crossing through which Judah and I had entered and left Gush Katif. They erected a yellow metal gate with the words in Hebrew and in English that it was now illegal for an Israeli to pass through (unless they were in possession of a press pass). A mobilisation of fifty-five thousand soldiers and police, the largest mass of troops since the Lebanon war, was deployed in seven circles in and around Gaza.

A few days earlier, Vicky and her family, all packed up, had left their house forever, together with most of the other residents of the secular settlement of Peat Sadeh. They had successfully done a deal with the Disengagement Authority and were being rehoused in a newly built development town called Mafki'im, south of Ashkelon inside Israel. Their new houses were not quite ready yet, so the government sent buses on the Thursday morning to take them for an all-expenses-paid two-week holiday in a Dead Sea resort, and they drove off to their new lives, clutching brochures advertising the stress-busting aromatherapy massages they would be entitled to, courtesy of the government.

Doron, the head of security, who had helped tow our car out of the sand dunes, together with four other families, had opted to go to another new development town in the same area called Nitzan, but stayed behind over the weekend to dismantle as much as he could of his house, even down to the window frames, not because he didn't want the Palestinians to have it, but because once he was in Nitzan, he planned to keep building. He was a man who just naturally liked putting up houses, that was the type he was.

Meir Rosenstein, who owned the boycotted electrical store, had bought a new house and new business up north in the Galilee. On the Thursday before the soldiers came, he loaded up the contents of his shop into a van and drove to Al-Mawasi, and sold off everything he had to the Palestinians, thumbing his nose at his former neighbours, whom he was going to the other end of the country to get away from.

On the same day, in Neve Dekalim, Judah found Miriam,

sitting on the kerb outside her closed-down coffee shop, sob-
bing her eyes out.

'What's the matter?' he asked her.

She had been left with thousands of shekels' worth of bad
debts from foreign correspondents who had run into the café,
grabbed a drink or some food and told her to put it on the tab.
They had never bothered to pay up.

The Sapersteins, true to their word, hadn't even so much as
packed a cup when the army arrived at dawn on the Monday
morning, going from house to house with eviction notices. I saw
Rachel interviewed several times on tv, spitting with rage. Their
only hope now was that there would turn out to be mass refusal
by the soldiers to obey orders, that the heartrending sight of
families being torn from their homes would melt the stony hearts
of the troops. Disgraceful scenes appeared on television, which
turned the stomachs of most Israelis – settlers calling the soldiers
Nazis, comparing their plight to that of the Jews in the Warsaw
Ghetto. One woman cut out orange stars from cloth and pinned
them to her children's clothing and made them walk out of the
house with their hands up, in imitation of that iconic photo of a
child in a cap with a yellow star on his chest, 'surrendering' to
the SS. These pieces of theatrics had the exact opposite effect of
that intended.

Some soldiers cried, all but a handful carried out their orders.
One officer in the army evicted his own son.

Now things were looking very serious indeed. The numbers of
residents of Gush Katif had dwindled; most had gone quietly. I
couldn't see Eran Sternberg anywhere on tv and there were no
quotes from him in the English-language Israeli media. Rachel
Saperstein and Eran's assistant Debbie Rosen reappeared, their
anger dissolving in tears: 'We've got nowhere to go,' they wailed,
'nothing has been prepared for us.'

Well, Debbie, I thought, you know perfectly well that the

reason you haven't got anywhere to go is that you boycotted the Disengagement Authority. You refused to believe it would happen. You turned your face against the future, and reality. Tough. I thought Debbie was a good woman, a nice person, but she was saturated with religious ideology turned political, she wandered around blindfolded and deluded. Vicky, Doron and Meir Rosenstein had read the future correctly, and prepared for it.

Moishe Saperstein, Rachel's husband, must have known – why hadn't he prepared her? She was talking now of moving to Hebron, the stronghold of the most radical, most extreme settlers in the whole of the occupied territories. Moishe rolled his eyes behind her back. I really hoped he would talk her out of it. I also wondered what was happening to his record collection, which contained the largest library of rare classical recordings in the country. Had he stood by and let the teenage conscripts, used to techno and hip hop blasting through the headphones of their iPods, sling LPs into boxes?

And where had Eran got to? Judah had a theory. The members of the Gush Katif regional council, which had organised the whole orange protest, were said to have secretly done a deal on their own behalf with the Disengagement Authority right back at the beginning of the whole process, and had already received and banked their cheques, amounting to around $200,000 per family. The poor saps like Debbie had been left in the dark. Debbie, her husband and children, and the Sapersteins were bussed out to three-star hotel rooms in Be'ersheva in the Negev.

I didn't see Ronni Bakshi either. I thought he might have been one of those who had barricaded themselves in the synagogue and had to be dragged out, one by one, kicking and screaming, but Judah said he thought not. His hunch was that the Bakshis had been the last to leave, on the Wednesday, before the final showdown. But they went quietly.

It was, as Vicky predicted, the infiltrators from the West Bank who were the last hold-outs. The government had gone to private contractors to lease the shipping containers to transport out of Gaza each settler's belongings. Right-wing West Bank firms had used the containers to smuggle the infiltrators in.

They enacted a last battle, hundreds of teenage girls piteously singing, entreating God to send them his miracle, while a few men took to the rooftops and poured an acid-like substance on the police and army below.

A woman set herself on fire in protest against the disengagement, and died of her burns a week or two later.

In a Druze town in Israel, a deserter from the army got on a bus and began to fire his gun, killing several passengers, until the others grabbed him and beat him to death. On the West Bank, a driver, a quiet family man with no record of holding fiery right-wing opinions, grabbed a gun from the security guard at a settlement and shot dead four nearby Palestinians in cold blood. They were his substitute, he said later, for Ariel Sharon.

The evacuation from Gaza and the four West Bank settlements took ten days from start to finish. By the end no one was left and the army started demolishing the houses, though not the homes and community centres, so that the Palestinian Authority could build high-density housing to relieve the overcrowding in the refugee camps.

For the religious settlers of Gush Katif the speed and ruthless efficiency of the evacuation, its inexorable rush to completion, the utter failure of every single one of their strategies to stop it – calling for a referendum, using the laws of the state, winning over the hearts and minds of Israelis, mass conscientious objection by the army – created a terrible theological crisis.

God had promised them the land of Israel, he had a covenant, a contract. All they had to do was live by his laws, and who could fault them? Yet the promised miracle did not come. Not even at the last moment, when they desperately, piteously prayed, rocking back and forth in their prayer shawls. This was the God who had parted the Red Sea to allow them to cross and escape the Egyptians, who had sent manna from heaven, who allowed Joshua's trumpet to crumble the very mortar that held together the stones of the city of Jericho. He made barren women fertile. He let people live eight hundred years. God could do anything he wanted to, and how could he not want the righteous settlers of Gaza to remain in their red-roofed homes? Did God actually want their houses to be handed over to the PA and their villages renamed, as they would be, after various Palestinian militants, such as the Hamas leader Sheikh Yassin?

'God will send a miracle,' a woman told me. 'I don't know what the miracle will be, but I know there will be one.'

And if the disengagement does happen? I had asked her.

'Then I will be very disappointed in God,' she said. I imagine that right now she must be giving him a piece of her mind.

Bu'ah

The novel I was trying to write in Israel was about a group of people who meet every week at a tango class in an unnamed city in the middle of a war. Every morning I worked, in the apartment on Ruppin Street; I was lost in my own world, as if I entered a dark cave every day, and when I walked along the beach in the afternoon (or early morning if it was hot), the people I passed, or sat down on a bench to watch – the woman who managed to lead a chaotic team of twenty or thirty cats in some sort of promenade; the men with scraggly ponytails drinking from paper-bagged bottles on the rocks behind the Dolphinarium where the Russian teenagers were killed; the man with the fat, amputated stumps energetically wheeling himself along the beachfront; the family from Ghana, dressed in their best clothes, walking hand-in-hand; the closely scarfed

women unpacking picnics on the sand at Alma beach and turning on their radios to play tinny Arabic music; the Russian
women sitting in a shady spot furtively exchanging a foreign
currency whose notes I couldn't manage to decipher; the beggar
who lay asleep, under a folded tent of cardboard, a scaly brown
open palm sticking out, pleading for coins; the woman in the
tweed skirt and embroidered white blouse with a worn face and
colourless hair who played the cello and ignored, contemptu-
ously, the one-shekel coins and lesser agorot that were thrown
at her; the mimes and children's clowns and performance artists
who began to arrange their bodies in various compromising
positions so that the parents of the children shielded their faces
with their hands and guided them away until someone called
the police and then there was a hue and cry about censorship
and living in a fascist state and an old man with bad dentures
pointed out that if you really lived in a fascist state you would-
n't be arguing with policemen about art – these individuals
sought citizenship of my inner city, and began to populate it,
and jostled for my attention.

What about Ramallah? What about Jenin and Nablus and
Bethlehem and Khan Younis and Rafah? What about the incursions, the targeted assassinations that killed not just their
quarry, but also innocent civilians, including children? What
about the stranglehold on towns, the checkpoints at which
people waited for hours in the boiling sun, miscarrying, going
into labour, newborn babies dying? What about ambulances
not being able to get through? What about stolen water? What
about humiliation? What about the difficulties faced by students trying to get an education? What about malnutrition?
What about the mental health problems a whole generation
was storing up for the future? How can you sit in an apartment
writing a novel when an hour's drive from your desk there is ter-

rible suffering experienced by real people, not people who exist on paper?

I could do it because that's what a writer does. Art gets made despite activism, not because of it.

But one day I received an invitation from Ora Ardun, a seventy-four-year-old Jerusalem woman whose grandparents had been part of the Second Aliyah, the emigration to Palestine of Jewish socialists who started the kibbutz system. *She* was an activist. She wanted me to accompany her to the *machsom*, the checkpoints, where a group of Israeli women went every day to monitor the activities of the army and she wanted me to write about it for the newspaper.

'My grandparents came from Odessa in 1905,' she said. 'They were idealists, they wanted to create a new Jew who would do moral work. The settlers call themselves Zionists, but they are not Zionists as far as the founders of the state were concerned. *I* am a Zionist, and this is why the checkpoints are a terrible blow to us Israelis as well as the Palestinians.

'My daughters are very unhappy – they think I am quite right to go to the checkpoints but they want someone else's mother to go. But I say that only by doing this can we reclaim the humanistic revolution of Zionism. We are calling on the world to help us reclaim our humanistic values.'

I asked Yael, my landlady, if she would come with me. She said yes, at once, but she took a different view about the world and its solidarity with the real Zionists. First of all, she didn't want her life story plastered all over the foreign press, although I had a million questions about it. What a life! And second, yes, she would come to the checkpoints but, 'I will not criticise my country abroad,' she said. 'I have enough work of this kind to do at home, without letting people abroad read what they want into what I say.'

We got a taxi to Jerusalem and on the way she told me how

she met her French husband when she was studying in Paris in the 1960s and was so homesick for Israel she would go into El Al offices just to hear her native language spoken. When she returned home for good she kissed the soil.

Ora said she was the real Zionist, but I thought Yael was Zionism incarnate, at least what my parents had meant by it. She was a Sabra, one of those mentally tough, proud, physically strong, sexy girls who had been in their teens in the first years of the state; the greatest generation, the socialists, the pioneers of free expression, the ones who had shaken off the ghosts and ghouls of *shtetl* life. The Yael generation knew *of* anti-Semitism, but had no experience of it. When she was a tiny girl of three years of age, her parents took her back to Lithuania, where she stood in the room, a miracle! A little child who spoke Hebrew aloud like a rabbi. They didn't come, those relatives; they stayed where they were, and were murdered.

When one of her sons went missing in Lebanon, during his army service, she told her other son to go and find him, and carry him home on his back if necessary. 'Go and find your brother,' she said to him. But, Mother— 'Go and find your brother.'

I can still hear the slight roll of the r and the short o in 'brother', and her eyes like anvils, striking sparks, as she said it.

'Now I don't love Israel so much,' she told me.

'Do you feel optimistic?' I asked her, after some kind of illusory progress had been made in the political process, which collapsed soon after.

'No. The Arabs hate us, and who can blame them after what we've done to them?'

The highway takes you east, past the airport, up through the Jerusalem hills, densely forested, the hills of the city capped with new Jewish suburbs, Arab towns to the left and right clearly distinguishable by their minarets. Then suddenly you reach the outskirts of the new city, West Jerusalem, and walking along the road, or standing at the bus stop, or hitchhiking, are the 'Dalmatians', the Orthodox Jews in black coats, black hats, black beards and white shirts.

The taxi enters the German Colony, an upper-middle-class neighbourhood built at the end of the nineteenth century by members of the Templar sect, which was founded in Germany in 1858 and whose members came to Palestine to escape religious persecution. Many of them were Nazi sympathisers during the Second World War, interned by the British and later repatriated to Germany or deported to Australia. The houses are really beautiful, built of the stone of the surrounding hills; this is one of the nicest parts of Israel if you dislike the shock of the new.

We arrived at the house of Hannah Barag and set off in her car. Hannah was sixty-eight. As we drove along she said that when she first went to the checkpoints a soldier called her a Palestinian whore. 'Listen,' she told him, 'with my looks and my age, do you think I still have a future in this profession?'

In a very few minutes, after passing the Hebrew University and the American Colony hotel, we reached Abu Dis. It is, or once was, a wealthy Palestinian town, a university town, close to the big city and with all the sophistication that entails. Large houses abutted the concrete wall that the Israeli government was building to keep out suicide bombers. I saw the Berlin Wall in the days just after the East German prison was opened, and it was high, but this was biblical in its conception, like the Tower of Babel, so immense that I suspected its builders harboured an ancient dream, a plan to keep going until it hit heaven, the roof of the world itself, creating a seamless barrier between the two peoples. It was also exceptionally ugly, made of giant concrete slabs lifted into place by cranes, and already, like the Berlin Wall, defaced with graffiti, comparing it to its East German predecessor and to the walls of the Warsaw Ghetto.

Yael looked up at it in disbelief. We had seen it on tv but real life was another matter. I watched her gazing up at its summit, and though she was a woman of erect bearing, she looked like a doll next to it.

If you are a Palestinian, the Zionist state must seem to you like a relentless military machine, cold, heartless, inhuman, ruthlessly efficient in its domination. I, on the other hand, had an entirely different view. During my time in Israel, my overriding impression of the government was that of incompetence and corruption, which manifested itself in almost every aspect of civilian and military life. Soldiers were left for weeks with no rations, until they began to mutiny. Strikes of public-sector workers left offices closed for months. Cabinet ministers' hands were in the till. A woman, Vicky Knafo, walked in the torrid heat of summer from Be'ersheva in the Negev desert all the way to Jerusalem with an Israeli flag round her shoulders, billowing behind her like a cloak, to camp outside the finance minister's office to protest against the vicious budgetary cuts that were going to force single mothers out to work. Fraud, corruption, arrogance, disorganisation, bureaucrats battling over petty fiefdoms, a cacophony of invective and racist hate speech even inside the Knesset . . . inside the regional super-power it seemed like a ramshackle Middle Eastern bazaar, the rules of the *balagan* pervading everything.

I had experienced a nasty shock of recognition when I read the final sentence of Antony Beevor's study of the end of the Third Reich, *Berlin: The Downfall*: 'The incompetence, the frenzied refusal to accept reality and the inhumanity of the Nazi regime were revealed all too clearly in its passing.' Let me make myself quite clear. I am morally disgusted by attempts to make any equivalence between Israel and Nazi Germany, Zionism and fascism. It is an analogy of mind-numbing laziness and spite, feeble-minded in its refusal to do the hard work of moving beyond moral outrage to rigorous analysis. 'Where are the gas chambers?' the Ramallah-based Israeli journalist Amira Hass asked the novelist José Saramago when he compared Gaza to Auschwitz. 'Not here, not yet,' he replied, smugly. In fiction, anything is possible; you can build gas chambers on the sand dunes of Gaza if you like, no one can or should stop you, this is the artist's freedom. He is free, too, to make a fool of himself when he lends himself to political activism, and we are equally free to demand that he develops some understanding of the history of the conflict he is actually dealing with, instead of the one that exists in his head. He says he has an inner truth, and that the artist's truth is greater than the vulgarity of that lesser form of language, 'facts', which are the grubby product of journalism. There is currently a war between truth and fact, between the artist and the reporter. This war rages inside me too, as someone who has practised, and continues to do so, both professions. 'Are you going to tell the truth?' I have been asked countless times by people I have interviewed. By which they mean, 'Are you going to tell *my* version of the story; will you transmit my own, inner truth?'

Facts frequently contain contradiction, muddle, disorder, paradox. They are not themselves an analysis, they are the material to build one. It is probably a universal characteristic of armies of occupation against a civilian population defending itself through guerrilla or terrorist tactics, that they collapse into ineptitude and casual brutality. There cannot be a battlefield doctrine where there is no battlefield, no formal divisions of tanks and terrain to be taken. It is the cruellest form of warfare, for both sides. That Israel's occupation was incompetent and corrupt, and that it became increasingly unable to look reality in the face, does not make it a Nazi regime, no more than the composition of a puddle being water makes it an ocean. All we can say is that they are both wet.

Here, at Abu Dis, the wall connected at a right angle with

another crumbling structure with a small high gap over which any agile person could easily climb. I could get across it, and I was at that time not very fit and rather clumsy and liable to put a foot wrong, and slip. On the other hand, if you were old, disabled, blind or carrying shopping or a baby, it was very hard to navigate. Later, I asked an officer in the army if he could explain to me what was the point of having a rupture in the wall that made life difficult for the most vulnerable people, and no impediment at all for the very individuals it had been purposely built to stop. Yossi Mendelevich wanted a barrier at Abu Dis. If there had been one, he had told me, then the murderer of his son Yuval would not have reached Haifa.

'Abu Dis is a problem,' the officer said, over breakfast in Tel Aviv the day before I left the country. 'To be honest, I am falling out of love with Israel.'

'Why?'

'The army lies. And so I have to lie too.' Eighteen months later he and his wife were gone, off to America. He was looking for a job on a local newspaper writing about college sports.

'The army lies,' Ora Ardun said. 'I didn't use to believe that, but I do now.'

We drove on to Qalandia, a town divided into two by the checkpoint. Beyond it lay Ramallah, the Tel Aviv of Palestine, the good-time city, the headquarters of the Palestinian Authority, and the place where it was possible to enter the Mercedes dealership and buy yourself a car if you had the money, and one can only assume that enough people did or it wouldn't have been there.

It was a bitterly cold day with high, blue skies. Every type of person and every class was standing in the line, waiting with their documentation: well-dressed businessmen in warm expensive coats; fashionable young women without headscarves; hard young men who could have wandered across a slit in space from a Puerto Rican neighbourhood of New York; teenage boys and girls laughing and flirting, hitting each other with bags of school books; women carrying babies in their arms because the roads are so rutted round the checkpoints that it is hard to wheel a child in a pushchair.

'It's very quiet today,' Hannah said, though to me there was a cacophony. She pointed at a fence a few metres away. 'Palestinian children throw stones at the soldiers and the soldiers fire back; a number of children have been killed here. It seems quiet now but when it gets dark it is more violent.'

Two volunteers, Phyllis and Tamar, were already at the checkpoint. Tamar was a type familiar to me from many other kinds of protest; you saw them at Greenham Common in Britain in the 1980s, trying to close down the American military base which had cruise missiles pointed at the Soviet Union; they were there in the 1990s standing in front of trucks transporting veal calves to the Continent; and in 2003 marching through the streets of London to stop the war in Iraq. They were from the 1960s generation of social and political protest, women whose values were formed by the idealism of those born during or just after the Second World War, the generation of feminism, pacifism, environmentalism, which finds the excesses of capitalism and globalisation repugnant and which is always prepared to put itself out to do something about it.

A Palestinian woman, holding a baby in her arms, stood in a black coat and stiletto-heeled boots, waiting. A small black scarf was stylishly knotted over her head, but it showed so much of her hair that it seemed more of a fashion statement than a symbol of modest Muslim womanhood. She contrasted sharply with Tamar, who was wearing tie-dye pants that could have been part of her wardrobe since 1967.

Tamar came running towards her and escorted her to the front of the queue. She approached a young female soldier, a teenage girl in grubby olive-green army uniform, her hair tied back from her pimply face. The soldier checked the woman's documents and let her pass. The woman with the baby and the high-heeled boots did not thank Tamar or smile at her. She hurried on, but her expression, as the dishevelled teenager checked her pass, displayed absolute contempt. She looked to me as if she should be shopping in Harrods, not standing on a rutted road outside Ramallah, forced to stand and wait and then be rescued by a Zionist peace activist with no sense of her own appearance, and a dirty little girl.

The women of Machsom Watch were the only Israelis most Palestinians had seen since the start of the intifada who are not in uniform, the only Israelis who exhibited human kindness, and sometimes that was enough to leave a favourable impression, even though the women often failed to succeed in persuading the soldiers to open a gate in the fence to let children through to school.

Others vented their anger against them because they were the only unarmed Israelis available to shout at. 'I tell them, you are at the wrong address,' Hannah said. 'But some tell us that we are no different, we are part of the same game.' When Ora told a group of Palestinians she was a peace activist, one cried out that he wanted war and not peace.

Ten days earlier, a woman suicide bomber at the Erez crossing at Gaza had managed to persuade a soldier that she was disabled and could not pass through the metal detector because of a metal plate in her leg. She killed four people and the Israeli radio phone-in shows were full of furious callers complaining that the Palestinians were abusing the pressure on commanders to treat women and children more humanely. 'That woman did a big disservice to her people and her own gender,' Ora said. 'It's the same as when they transported military equipment in ambulances.'

My mind was still full of Yuval, under his granite headstone on the quiet hill overlooking the sea on the lower slopes of Mount Carmel. On his behalf, I asked her what she felt about the possibility that she would abet a suicide bomber passing through a checkpoint. 'I can't say I've never thought of it,' she replied, 'but if you sit on a jury you have the same dilemma. Look.'

She pointed to a small hill beyond the checkpoint.

'So?' I said.

'We call it Tora Bora. It is easy to pass across that way.'

And then it became blindingly obvious that the checkpoints were not there to prevent suicide bombers entering Israel. Ora understood checkpoints very well. At the age of thirteen she was a radio operator in the Haganah, the Jewish militias opposing British Mandate rule in Palestine. She was smuggling radio parts and no one stopped her because she was so small and so young. During the war of independence in 1948 she was a corporal. It was, she said, a just war. But what was happening at the *machsom* was nothing to do with justice or war, it was a system of structured humiliation.

At the Qalandia checkpoint I saw a lot of international journalists and political activists entering and leaving Ramallah. I suddenly realised that this was the place to be, here was the spot on the planet where history was happening, where the news we saw back home on tv was being made; if you wanted to be where the zeitgeist was, you would go to Ramallah, and I was going home, to Tel Aviv, turning my back on reality.

Most mornings I had coffee at a tiny café on Ben Yehuda Street that doesn't exist any more – the owners didn't pay their taxes and were forced to close down. I liked talking to the kid who ran it for them, Ma'or (the name means 'illuminated', from God's primal injunction 'Let there be light'), a skinny surfer from one of the working-class towns in the interior, near the airport. His mother was from Turkey, his father from Spain. His dad had died just before he went into the army; he had been sick for a long time, and when he could no longer go out to work as an electrician, Ma'or would help him assemble light switches at home, on piece work. Ma'or went off to the navy in a cute white uniform, fixing ships, travelling up and down the coast between the naval bases at Haifa and Ashkelon, until he got tired of all the travelling and went AWOL, and when they caught up with him, he sat in a military jail for a few days. He told the story really well, and made me laugh.

He lived to surf. You been surfing today? I asked him. He looked at me as if I was mad. 'It's cold,' he said. 'I'm a Jew, you think I like to suffer?'

He had a redheaded girlfriend (she was a sales assistant in the clothes store Mango) who used to be a dancer until she went into the army and gained several kilos on stodgy army food, 'and now I dance with the cakes,' she said, putting a fork into a piece of pastry. She wanted to become a teacher or a social worker. Ma'or was so proud of her – a guy like him had got a superior, red-haired Ashkenazi girl like her. 'There's a lot of rubbish out there,' he said, very seriously, looking at me with his blue eyes.

One time I asked him my favourite question, the one I had put to Cabinet ministers and novelists, rabbis and taxi drivers.

'What is a Jew, Ma'or?'

He nodded, and stroked his goatee beard. He was enormously interested in his hair. A barber up the street had hacked off his ponytail when all he asked for was a trim. He was absolutely livid. He had pictures from fashion magazines of the style he had wanted and had shown the barber, and he showed them to me. 'Does this' – points at his head – 'look *anything* like this?'

I'm waiting to hear what Ma'or has to say to the most puzzling question that can beset a Jew.

'The Jew is an experiment,' Ma'or said. 'He is the first human being. God wanted to know what happens when you do this to a Jew, what happens when you do that. He tries everything on us first.'

If I can give any reason other than the original purpose for my coming to Tel Aviv, which was to write, for my being in the little patisserie on Ben Yehuda instead of Ramallah or Khan Younis, it was because of this conversation. I came to the country as a Jew, to try to understand Jews in the place where they were most densely concentrated.

Understanding them on several levels, of course. I was sitting in the little café with my cappuccino reading the newspaper, reading of the latest sickening killings of Palestinian civilians taking place a few kilometres away, or that 20 per cent of Israeli children were living below the poverty line, or that army social workers spent all their time dealing with soldiers who had nowhere to go on weekend leave because their parents were homeless . . . and I would look up to see what Ma'or and his girlfriend or the men who sat there drinking coffee before going to work were saying, trying to snatch a few words of a language I don't understand, and a few of those words would indeed detach themselves and float through the air to me. 'Eyal Berkovic . . . Kevin Keegan . . . Manchester City . . . Portsmouth.'

I would turn to the sports pages and find the story that was so exercising them. Berkovic, Israel's top footballer, having had a row with Kevin Keegan, the Manchester City manager, had moved to Portsmouth . . .

I was in the *bu'ah*. The bubble.

To tolerate life in Israel during the second intifada, to deal with *hamatzav*, the situation, and the *balagan* of existence, it was necessary to create your own world.

There was a little suicide bombing while I was there, at Petah Tikvah, where Ma'or and his girlfriend lived. I saw her bent over the newspaper, tears in her eyes. The girl who had been killed, her own age, had been standing at the bus stop when the suicide bomber tried to get on the bus, didn't manage it, and detonated himself.

Suicide bombings made small, self-enclosed worlds consisting of family, a few friends and a tiny geography. You go to *this* supermarket which is not in a busy mall, *this* café which has an armed guard (or, like the one I went to, was too small to be a viable target because not enough people could be killed), you drive your kids to school along *this* side road which isn't a bus route, and to hell with anyone you don't know or trust. This is your own personal *bu'ah*, and no one who is not in it is above suspicion.

When I first came to Tel Aviv I had political conversations all the time. After a couple of months I found that we talked of other things. I tried to understand what had changed and realised it was me, I had changed. We had talked about politics because I raised the subject. Once I stopped, no one else took over that role. I had made my own *bu'ah*.

What was happening in Gaza or Nablus – the curfews, the checkpoints, the terrifying incursions of troops, the targeted assassinations, the collapse of the social infrastructure, the malnutrition, the cages in which Palestinians were fenced off, like zoo animals – could be happening in Bosnia, instead of a twenty-five-minute drive away, because no one went there except your son the soldier, or your husband the reservist, and they didn't talk about what they had seen because they couldn't; they didn't have the emotional language to express it – who among us does? The soldier comes home and gratefully re-enters his *bu'ah*.

During the Gaza disengagement, Israeli journalists spent a day walking up and down Shenkin Street, asking the young people there what they thought of the scenes on tv, of settlers being dragged from their homes. One girl said she didn't know anything about it, she never read any newspapers or watched the news. 'I've got my own problems,' she said. The rest said they didn't care, weren't interested. While Debbie Rosen wept and Rachel Saperstein screamed, and the woman set fire to herself in protest, Tel Aviv was at the beach.

Israeli businessmen invested in escapism, the *bu'ah's* wall-paper: foreign travel, home decor, kitchen equipment, the National Geographic channel on tv for the rich, soap operas and Spanish 'telenovellas' for the poor.

As if the government was simply a caretaker, changing the light bulbs, vacuuming the floors, it no longer had any mean-ingful connection to the mass of the population. 'How did you vote in the last election?' I asked Ma'or.

'I didn't. Who was there to vote for?'

But there were always tears in the *bu'ah*. What entered it was refracted from Gaza and Ramallah and did not shed any light on what was happening there but on what was happening to Israel itself. It was a society floating on boiling anger, fear, anxiety, post-traumatic shock, aversion, brutality. You saw it in the road rage, in the domestic violence, in the rape, the desire to build walls against not just suicide bombers but your own neighbours. The country was covered with walls and fences, dividing towns and neighbourhoods. Suspicion, fear, exploding psycho-dramas detonating whole families. I would be woken in the night by ter-rible screams, the raised voices of husbands and wives, the sound of objects smashing against walls, the police sirens. Or on the street, screeching tyres, sickening metal collisions, tirades of fury between drivers. Hair-trigger tempers. Horrible sorrow behind closed doors.

And also, infuriatingly, ordinary life, which has the power to persist, come what may, because what we think of as 'nothing' is so important that it insists on intruding everywhere. The close examination of the sports pages. The queue outside the cinema for the latest Hollywood film. Weddings. A child's first day at school. A graduation ceremony. Gay Pride day.

A Lithuanian doctor, her head bent over her studies, completing the gruelling course that will qualify her as a paediatrician. A Russian computer expert driving into the desert to photograph the ibex. His wife in her lab advancing some medical breakthrough. A father, whose son has been diagnosed with Attention Deficit Disorder, experiments on himself with Ritalin before he will give it to his boy. A baker writes out the recipe for a flour-free Passover cake which his grandmother brought with her from Morocco. In the Jersualem hills vineyard owners receive the news that they are to receive a recommendation from the Torah and Talmud of wine writers, Hugh Johnson. A man who runs a stationery shop is training for a half marathon. People fall in love, sometimes it works out, other times it doesn't.

And I'm in the apartment, standing stock still, terror coursing through me, acids building up inside my system, heart banging like a hammer, my head feels like it will explode, or maybe I have to run to the bathroom and be sick, throw up in the nearest receptacle, because the Blaster Worm virus has destroyed the hard drive on my laptop and I am waiting for Yan to drive me and it to Rehovot to a computer store to see what if anything can be salvaged from the worst *balagan* any writer can imagine.

This was my *bu'ah*.

Sifrut

'You can write with your head, you can write with your heart, or you can write with your whole being,' said the small man with the quiet voice, the bald head and the glasses, a combination which he made a quiet joke of, and the green eyes that looked at me with curiosity, listening to what I said, not speaking much himself, though what he had to say you wanted to pay close attention to. So I abandoned the novel I had started to write and embarked, instead, on something else, but this something else – this novel about a fictional city, because there was a city inside me that begged to be written about, which was not the Tel Aviv of the Tel Avivians who lived in it, but my own hometown, the hometown of the soul, if you want to get spiritual about it, or whatever the soul means – this novel which was of my whole being proved a total terror to actually write.

I met Aharon Appelfeld twice in the restaurant in Ticho House in Jerusalem where he goes every day to work, and again, after my return home, when he came to London and we drove to Bath together, with his wife, to give a talk at a literary festival. These conversations are among the most intense, the most exciting and the most troubling I have ever had, which is really saying a lot because immediately after the second meeting we were joined by the novelist David Grossman, and Aharon left, and David and I talked and he also is some talker.

There was something else Aharon said, a habit I have been trying to learn ever since, which is that when a person speaks with great passion or anger or intensity, pay attention not to the subject, but to the emotion behind the words. If I could do this, then the endless, insoluble debate about the rights and wrongs of the Israeli–Palestinian conflict, according to whom you were talking, would fall away, and you would come to understand a different truth, which would compel you to address what matters to them, and why.

Appelfeld's novel, *Badenheim 1939*, had never left hold of me since I read it a few years ago. It is an allegory of the ghetto: a group of artists find themselves in a music festival town (Salzburg?) increasingly cut off from the rest of the world. They squabble and ignore the obvious evidence before their eyes. What do they think the inspectors of the Sanitation Department are doing, who 'now spread all over the town. They took measurements, put up fences, and planted flags. Porters unloaded rolls of barbed wire, cement pillars, and all kinds of appliances, suggestive of preparations for a public celebration.'

People come, no one leaves. The artists sink into melancholy and inertia. All the new arrivals are Jews, someone remarks, but no one makes much of this coincidence. The situation deteriorates imperceptibly, by slow degrees; the windows of the grand hotel are darkened by overgrown vines; food grows scarcer; the fish in the hotel aquarium begin to starve and die.

The inhabitants, who by now are inmates, hear that they are being transferred 'east' and wonder if their pensions will be going with them, and whether they will be able to live quite prosperously in the cheaper lands beyond the civilised borders of central Europe. On the last page, they assemble at the railway station, and after a long wait in which they buy lemonade and other refreshments from the kiosk:

> An engine, an engine coupled to four filthy freight cars, emerged from the hills and stopped at the station. Its appearance was as sudden as if it had risen from a pit in the ground. 'Get in!' yelled invisible voices. And the people were sucked in. Even those who were standing with a bottle of lemonade in their hands, a bar of chocolate, the head-waiter with his dog – they were all sucked in as easily as grains of wheat poured into a funnel. Nevertheless Dr. Pappenheim found time to make the following remark: 'If the coaches are so dirty it must mean that we have not far to go.'

Many Jews in Germany, particularly those in the middle and upper classes, the most assimilated, as Appelfeld's parents were, chose to ignore every warning sign. Believing that Hitler was a vulgar buffoon, they assumed that fascism was a passing phenomenon. They placed their faith in the intelligence and cultural superiority of the German people of which they felt themselves to be a full and patriotic part, fighting in their wars and wearing the Iron Crosses of the nation with pride. These German middle classes, the most assimilated Jews in the world (even more so than the Jews of America), who said that they were German first and Jewish a very distant last, were the least

Zionist Jews of all. They insisted on their right to remain in the Diaspora, barely acknowledging that there was such a thing, for they were nationalists to their core, German nationalists, and they believed in the state and its institutions. In Palestine the German refugees would become known as Yekkes, from the word for jacket, because even in the intense heat of the Middle East they refused to abandon formal dress*. They were rational, optimistic, secular, obedient and without that paranoia that characterised so much of eastern European Jewish life. Perhaps it was rerouted and manifested itself in hypochondria and the various hysterias that Freud had diagnosed in the Viennese Jewish bourgeoisie.

The *Ostjuden*, the Jews of the East (my Jews, the kind I am descended from), the rabble from the *shtetls* of Poland and the Russian Pale of Settlement, the fish sellers and butchers, the rag-tag rabbis and the bullet-headed gangsters, knew different. They had grown up amongst hostile neighbours and their instincts were to believe that the *goyem* hated Jews enough to want to kill them.

It is that sense of bourgeois denial that Appelfeld was trying to write about in *Badenheim 1939*, of people who neither passively accepted their fate, nor fought back, because they could not, or would not, alter their view of Germany and its civilising influences, temporarily in abeyance, but sure to return. They did not believe there was such a thing any more as anti-Semitism, or if there was, it was a complaint of those who chose to live in ways that made them conspicuous: attending synagogues, muttering in a mongrel tongue, wearing outlandish clothes, sticking together,

---

*But also, according to Judah Passow, it is an acronym of *Yehudi kasheh yediah* – Jews who have difficulty understanding. Understanding where they were and what was going on in this new country so far away from Central European rationality and decorum.

turning their backs against modernity. These low-life types would, they believed, inevitably die out as the century proceeded.

When Appelfeld began to write in the 1950s, there was in Israel and elsewhere a hostile critical reaction to anyone who wanted to create literature – *sifrut* – out of the Holocaust. The facts themselves were still being established; there was unfinished business with war criminals like Adolph Eichmann, the architect of the Final Solution, and Dr Mengele, the conductor of outlandish medical experiments, still on the loose. If one had anything to say, it should be written down in plain, straightforward, unvarnished language, or if you did bother with that literary nonsense, then you should dramatise the deeds of the ghetto fighters, the socialists or the partisans. For Israel, in the early years of the state, was determined to bury the past. Few people spoke of their experiences at all, and when they did, they were usually told to shut up. Zionism, the existence of a Jewish country with its own army, was the antidote to the men and women who went like sheep to the slaughter. It required simple, uncomplicated people who knew which end of a gun you hold and which end the bullets come out of.

Appelfeld was a fourteen-year-old boy in 1946 when he arrived in Palestine from a Displaced Persons camp in Italy. At the outbreak of the war, the Germans had marched into Chernowitz, one of those border towns of eastern Europe that are always changing hands. There is a marvellous photograph of him, a spoilt smooth-faced child pictured on a rocking horse in a sailor suit. If there had been no Hitler, no Nazi Party, no war, no Holocaust, who would that child have grown up into? Suppose the first half of the century had been placid and mildly, liberally progressive, inching forwards by degrees to a middling prosperity and social democracy, no sudden rash big ideas – then there would still be a Jewish eastern Europe, a great mass of the

Jewish people living in the same places they had inhabited for a thousand years. As the century advanced, peacefully, the life of the *shtetl* would have been transformed by the usual changes that were taking place everywhere. A man might sit in the Jewish town of Chelm, with synagogues and cemeteries where the bones of his ancestors lay buried beneath Hebrew letters engraved in stone, and send in Yiddish an email to his uncle in Minsk forwarding an interesting newspaper article about the fall in high-tech share prices or a file attachment with a photo of Jennifer Aniston.

One day I walked into a café on a freezing cold, rainy lunchtime in Tel Aviv, and sat down to order a bowl of chicken soup with a side of chopped liver. Most of the few tables had been pushed together for a party, a group of old people, the men in suits and ties, the women in skirts and blouses and gold necklaces and bracelets, all eating and spitting and scratching their ears and blowing their noses and talking in Russian.

Everyone sitting round that table looked identical to my aunts and uncles on my mother's side, the same faces, the same short round shape, the same hairstyles even, because these were clearly new arrivals to Israel, and they dressed as they had done back home. I thought, if you pricked us and took a drop of our blood to analyse it, theirs and mine, you may well prove that we were indeed related, and that this was a branch of my family, distant cousins perhaps, who had stayed behind in the region of Kiev when my mother's parents, like my father's, bought those trick tickets that took you not to America but England. There was me, speaking English, reading English, my head full of the kings and queens of England and the Chartists and a few names of English wildflowers; and there they were, tipped over into the twenty-first century, full of bad memories and pictures in their family albums of aunts murdered in camps and uncles dead in the snow somewhere outside Stalingrad.

The day the Germans arrived in Chernowitz, Aharon's mother, who was out on the streets, was shot. He and his father were deported to a camp. A family that had relied on servants was barely even a family. At the age of eight he escaped the camp and spent the years of the war alone, rarely speaking. He survived for three years by staying on the edges of the towns and villages in the forests of the Ukraine, among thieves and prostitutes, until he was adopted as a kind of mascot by a troop of Red Army soldiers who put him to work as a cook. When he arrived in Palestine he had a smattering of many languages but was barely able to talk. He had only had a year of school.

The early years of Israel were full of these orphaned children, whom nobody knew anything about and were themselves without anything that could anchor them to a society, apart from certain rituals such as their induction into the army. Too young to remember what it was they might go back to, even if it were possible to do so (a thousand Jews who attempted to return to their former homes in Poland were murdered after the end of the war, by Poles), they were forced to create new selves, out of nothing but themselves.

Memory was trauma, and memory was all they had, primal memories of a type it is impossible to forget. The face of Appelfeld's mother, her shape and smell and voice, these were lodged inside him, and he could no more remove them and live than he could cut out his own heart and live.

There were thousands of survivors in Israel, who ran the clubs and organisations that tried to weave out of the great holes in families a new network of intimacy. Their relationship with the places they had come from was that of longing, and also revulsion.

No one asked the children what they remembered, because it was assumed that they were too young to have anything to remember, or if they did, a child forgets, and anyway, their recollections were uninspiring babyish stuff compared to the concrete past of these who had been 'sucked in as easily as grains of wheat poured into a funnel', who before the war had jobs and street addresses, had had a life entire, fully furnished. A weekly radio programme* consisted of heartrending messages in which survivors enquired after lost family and friends, lists of names read out, in case someone recognised them and a reunion could be arranged. The children who arrived alone in Palestine had nobody, knew nobody, and some were so young they could not even tell you their own names or the name of the town where they had been born. They were nobody. Often mute.

I had already written a novel about the war between past and future, that impulse in the emerging Israeli psyche, even before the creation of the state, to amputate everything that had gone before out of an optimistic belief that it was possible to remake the human race, and the Jew more than most, completely restructured. This bitter struggle, dreadfully resented (particularly by the Jews who would arrive from the Mediterranean and Middle Eastern lands of North Africa, Iran, Iraq, Yemen, Syria), had its origins in the very first idea of Zionism, among the rival claims to the language of the new country: should it be Yiddish, the demotic tongue of the Diaspora, a mongrel dialect of medieval German and smatterings of Hebrew, tainted by its associations with persecution and passive acceptance of suffering? Or Hebrew itself, rescued from the department of dead languages, the very words they spoke at Masada and other historic moments when the Jews fought back? Others suggested German, the language of the new century's modernity, of science and philosophy. No one suggested Ladino, the Sephardic tongue, or Arabic, the language that was spoken not just by the neighbours but by the Sephardi themselves.

*Still transmitting in 1980, when Yan and Rosita arrived in Israel.

On the kibbutzim, the socialists who came from Russia, and sat under the date palms arguing about Marx, Engels and Lenin, believed that the new Jew would neither labour for others, nor rely on others' labour, setting, fatally, in stone their separation from the Arabs, whom contemporary writings picture as a quaint backdrop to the ongoing struggle to drain swamps and plant oranges: feudal, backward and, like the Jews of *shtetl* Europe, limited by a supernatural adherence to religious ritual. While the Arabs were lying prone on carpets in their mosques, praying, the Zionists thought of themselves as forging into the future, bringing to the benighted lands of the Levant every new idea they could lay their hands on. Modernity and progressive thought, it would turn out, was itself a form of colonialism, just like the railways laid down by the British in nineteenth-century India, but in their innocence (and they seem to me very innocent indeed), they did not understand that. They were among the least postmodern people ever to have walked the planet.

Meanwhile, postwar Israeli society was harsh towards the survivors (perhaps shame was at the bottom of it), and for their part, not urged to speak, they remained silent, to try to forget.

But for Appelfeld, art could *only* come from memory. If it was true, as he said, that to create real art you must write with your whole being, the being that he was – the deepest part of his being – had been formed by the intense memories of his mother before the war; the horror of her brutal, sudden murder; the endless trudge along an icy road, holding the hand of his father; the casual atrocities of the camp; the fear and loneliness in the Ukrainian forest; the war's end, the rag-tag army of children wandering through Europe, almost feral now; the perverts and unscrupulous conmen who preyed on them, the ones who took the most gifted, the prodigies, and turned them into performing animals for their master's profit.

'It was not from a pleasant man that I learned to pray,' Appelfeld wrote in his memoir, *The Story of a Life*. His parents were not religious people; they sneered at their own parents' primitive superstitions. He did not know even the rudiments of Judaism, and when, in the transit camp en route to Palestine after the war, where 'Men played cards, drank vodka and had sex with women in broad daylight', in certain dark corners a few people, but not many, prayed.

Appelfeld wanted to pray, but did not know how. Each time he asked to be taught how to pray, he was rebuffed; one man told him: 'You'll be sailing to Palestine soon . . . In Palestine they work on kibbutzim and they don't pray.'

He did find a teacher, one who slapped him every time he made a mistake; sometimes, the boy thought, 'he was hitting me in order to uproot my desire to pray'.

I have read this short chapter of his memoir, *The Story of a Life*, many times, and on each occasion that I open the book and see those words – 'It was not from a pleasant man that I learned to pray' – I feel the same shock, as if it was me that had been slapped. For to pray is to attempt to make a direct and personal connection with God himself, the small self speaking to the divine. A man who teaches another to pray must be infused with goodness, or at least good intent. The person who taught Appelfeld to pray eventually received a visa for Australia and departed, carrying a bottle of black-market liquor. Appelfeld remained behind, for a while, praying with the others, until one of them suggested that he smuggle cigarettes into Sicily and, when he refused, threatened him. From then on he stopped praying, was moved to another camp 'and my desire to pray was sent into hiding'.

I am very fortunate that while it was not a pleasant man who taught him to pray, it was a pleasant man – himself – who taught me what literature is.

*

'Like evil spirits, people who know it all seem to be everywhere,' he writes.

I had already become suspicious of isms and ologies, and he confirmed that during the war there were communists 'who preached equality and the love of one's fellow man in the town squares [who] turned into beasts when truly tested. But there were also communists for whom the belief in their fellow man became so purified that up close they seemed like religious people . . . There were those who followed Jewish traditions but whom the war made heartless and selfish; and there were those who elevated God's commandments to ever higher degrees of light.'

Appelfeld had seen life, during the war, 'naked and unadorned'. All of it, he wrote, 'the good and the bad, the beautiful and the ugly – all these were revealed . . . as strands of the same rope. Thank God it didn't turn me into a moralist. On the contrary, I learned how to respect human weakness and how to love it, for weakness is our essence and our humanity.'

The Israelis on that block of Ben Yehuda where I lived; or the ones in uniform in the paratroopers camp; or the ones with the eyes of fanatics, blazing, in the settler enclave in Gush Katif; or the ones who were not Israelis, but Palestinians, waiting to have their documents examined at the checkpoint in Qalandia – none of them were villains or heroes, but for the most part ordinary people filled with greed, stupidity, longing, envy, kindness, humour, shallowness, profundity, intelligence, cowardice, insensitivity, alertness, vacuity, keen penetration, insipid, intense, beautiful, vain, ugly, self-absorbed, unselfconscious, pompous, plain-speaking, quiet, meek, bullying, brave, weak, religious, faithless, near death or on the brink of new life. If we are to believe Edgar Reitz's film *Heimat*, or the accounts of the rape by Soviet soldiers of the women of the city during the fall of Berlin, the same seems to be true of the civilian population of Nazi Germany.

On my return to London, people asked me what had changed in my point of view. It was easy to answer, 'Nothing.' That is, understanding what they meant by 'point of view', I said I could see no viable solution to the conflict that did not have as its conclusion two states, dwelling within legal, negotiated borders, one Jewish, one Palestinian, with the matter of the right of return of refugees settled by an agreed formula of recognition and compensation.

I was much more wary than I was before of words like 'apartheid', 'colonialist' and 'terrorist'. I was even more resistant than I was before to using language that was formed out of taking common words and adding a suffix that politicised them. I gained a deeper understanding, perhaps a crippling one, of the difficulties that confront a writer; I lost my ease with my own profession. 'Words are powerless when confronted by catastrophe,' Appelfeld wrote, 'they're pitiable, wretched, and easily distorted. Even ancient prayers are powerless in the face of disaster.'

'I have no words to describe the agony,' said Yossi Mendelevich.

After his first novel, *Smoke*, was published, in 1962, Appelfeld was summoned by the right-wing Israeli poet Uri Zvi Greenberg who wanted to tell him what he thought of his little book, a tirade of criticism not just against his own work but against the whole intellectual enterprise in Israel at that time. Greenberg told him that the Jews' gift from the Creator was that of vision and prophecy. The individual was not the point. '"The collective must precede him," Greenberg shouted, "because the collective is what creates language, culture and the belief system. If the individual makes his contribution to the collective, he raises the level of the collective and that of himself too. A creative person who does not do this will not be included in the nation's memory."'

To be fair to Greenberg, he was one of those who from its early days had been forming a new national literature in what was effectively a new language. On the other side of the political divide were other artists who were busy with a new Palestinian art, which also reflected the collective, stamped by a yearning for lands lost, for return, for pride and dignity and freedom from occupation.

Contemporary readers make great, perhaps intolerable demands of literature; they require it more and more to bear witness, to conform to the work of journalists, to make a moral case. People are always asking writers if they think that art can change the world; journalists believe that their craft can and should, and set out to do so.

What is a writer without a conscience? Israel and Palestine are flooded with visitors from abroad who take a vacation from the solitude of literary creation and go to the public square, where you have to shout to make yourself heard above the babble of voices, and what you say sounds crude and even coarse when you see it in print and are no longer shaking with strong emotion.

Now this was my dilemma as a writer. I did not think that literature should make a statement. In fact, I thought the exact opposite: that it should create ambiguity, doubt, discomfort, confusion. At the end of reading a novel or a poem, you should feel that your mind is chaos – at least, this is what reading good literature does for me. Just before I went to Israel, that summer, I read Vasily Grossman's novel *Life and Fate*, set in Leningrad during the Second World War, the *War and Peace* of the Soviet Union. It took me three weeks to read and three weeks to recover from the experience of reading it. At the end of that period, any lingering feeling that communism was a good idea lay dead and buried. What was left from the vast wreckage of that social, political and economic experiment was a couple of small/big things: kindness, empathy. Appelfeld had shown me that good and bad people went into the camps and good and bad were tested in them, and good and bad survived, came out, went their separate ways, some to Palestine, and the new state consisted of those who were kind and those who were not. *Shtarkers*, *menshes*, *schlemiels*, all of them were there. Israel was not a country made up of Primo Levis' possessed of penetrating insight into the nature of morality, but a wild combination of all types, including 'bald people, with glasses'.

There were Israelis who believed that the Arabs should be expelled from the land, were prepared to walk into a mosque with an automatic weapon and gun them down if necessary. There were also Israelis (one or two) who believed that the Jews were, in that shadowy way of theirs, plotting to take control of the world, and thought that there should be a real debate about the authenticity of the Tsarist anti-Semitic forgery, the *Protocols of the Elders of Zion*. Israelis who, as a friend drily remarked, 'carry the Jewish suicide gene'.

And here was my problem: for as any writer knows, the novel is about the individual, his fears and weaknesses. Yet what had compelled me to write my novel was not the individual, but the collective, the puzzling troubling question of the Jewish collective. What was a Jew?

Why ask? Because the whole idea of it fascinates me, because I want to know why people behave the way they do, and I can't reject out of hand the idea that this infuriating, argumentative, *davkaesque* quality of the people of Israel, and indeed myself, comes down to something that reaches back through millennia, beyond history, to one of the world's great stories.

Of a man standing on a mountain arguing with God. And perhaps every work of *sifrut*, literature, is that original dispute re-enacted between the author and reality (*metziyut*), to try to deny it, to blaspheme, to say, 'It is not true, you haven't created *everything*. Let me show you what I can do . . .' And then you try, and one time in a million it comes to something.

And so you're back with the shortest stories of all, like this one, about a lecturer who stands at the podium and begins his remarks by telling the audience, 'The essence of Judaism is disputation,' at which a voice responds, 'I beg to differ.'

Lashuv

At the end of my four-month stay in Israel, I felt that I had got to the bottom of one thing, one small aspect of that society, its most baffling, maddening, contradictory puzzle. Why did they behave like that?

When two of the entrants to the *davka* contest pointed out that the origins of the word were Aramaic, it occurred to me that this characteristic of the Jews, to do something in spite of, and even to spite – themselves and others – might be not just older than the state of Israel, or even older than the Diaspora, but absolutely encoded into the primal identity of the Jewish people. The quality of being stiff-necked, which so irritated God, reminded me a great deal of the discussions I had had on the finer nuances of *davka* which implied a principled stubbornness, a persistence in behaviour that was cutting your nose off to spite your face. When I emailed Judah to ask him where his entry in the *davka* contest was, having already received the one from his father, who had been one of those who supplied the Aramaic origin, Judah replied: 'If my father's involved in this *davka* contest, *davka* I don't want to have anything to do with it.' Meaning, I can't beat him on scholarship, so I don't want to enter, despite the temptation of a pair of glasses that turn Chanukah into Christmas.

On occasion, I have gone into a café, ordered something, waited and waited and waited, and, on enquiring where my order is, been told by the waitress that she is really sorry but the kitchen lost it. But they will start right now and it will be with me in just a few minutes. At this, I become so irate that I tell her no, I'm leaving, I'm going to go to another café and start all over again – looking for a table, reading the menu, making my selection, trying to attract the attention of one of the waiting staff . . . none of which makes sense because I just have to sit at *this* table a few more minutes and my food will be there, but it's the principle of the thing. *Davka* I won't sit here another minute.

When seen from the outside, reading the newspapers and watching tv, the attitude of Israeli politicians and indeed the voting public was inexplicable particularly from the vantage point of progressive opinion in Europe. This was because outside opinion was subject to an application of rationality devoid of the *davka* principle.

Why had the Israeli electorate kicked out Ehud Barak right in the middle of negotiations at Taba, when the European press agreed that the two sides were really close and it would have taken only a few more days and perhaps they could have reached an agreement? Why – at that historic moment – had a general election been called and the people voted in Ariel Sharon, the butcher of Beirut, whom even David ben Gurion, the first prime

minister, had called a serial liar, a man the Israeli court system
had judged not fit to hold office?

The answer was: If the Palestinians go starting an intifada in
the middle of negotiations, *davka*, let's show 'em. ('I asked him to
lend me his bicycle for a ride, and this bastard has done *davka*.
Slapped me a few, too.')

To stretch *davka* to its most obvious conclusion, one only had
to look at the situation Israel was in under international law. It
seemed blindingly obvious to me that if Israel wanted to remain
a Jewish state and not drift into world-wide pariah status, it would
have to give up the occupied territories and settle the matters of
Jerusalem and the rights of Palestinian refugees. Were it not to do
so, it would not survive, but it was possible *davka* that it would not
do any of those things, and would indeed not survive.

When you presented the impeccable logic of this to Israelis,
what you got was an argument. They would argue over every last
millimetre of international law. They subjected it to microscopic
scrutiny looking for legal loopholes, as if they were tax lawyers
with a crooked client. The range of public opinion among
Israelis was absolutely breathtaking. A guide book had noted
that there was no point in losing your temper with Israelis to
make them back down from some outrageous behaviour as this
would be the signal to start an argument, and there was nothing
that the average Israeli relished more.

Davka and *chutzpah*, the outrageous cheek that allowed Israel
constantly to try it on with other world leaders, to take things
as far as they thought they could get away with, such as the
policy of establishing 'facts on the ground', were the condition
of the people: complicated, intense, argumentative, often self-
defeating.

I was trying to tell someone about this idea of mine, for this
book, the one you are reading, and he interrupted with a joke.
That's it, I said. That's the place in a nutshell.

A man comes home from work on night shift, goes straight upstairs to the bedroom and finds his wife lying in a seductive pose under the sheet.

He gets into bed and begins to make love to her. After he's finished, feeling hungry, he goes downstairs to the kitchen and finds his wife eating breakfast. 'How did you get down here so fast?' he asks her.

'What do you mean? I've been here for half an hour.'

'Well, who's that upstairs in our bedroom that I've just had sex with?'

'Oh my god, you've just done it with my mother!'

She runs upstairs and finds her mother lying in shock in the bed. 'Mother,' she cries, 'when he got into bed with you, why didn't you say something?'

'I've not spoken to that son-of-a-bitch for fifteen years, *davka* I should start now?'

This is a book about Israelis, about what I know about them, and there is another book to be written, about Palestinians and what someone else knows about them. That book will tell a story of return, of what it means, of how it is embedded in Palestinian identity. No return, no peace, Palestinians told me.

I left Israel, on 31 January 2004, burdened by a sense of horror, for a thought had occurred to me that was unbearable: that at its heart, indeed because of what is in the hearts of its people, not just its leaders, this conflict might be insoluble.

After four months in Israel and hundreds of hours of conversations, I found not a scrap of evidence that Jewish Israelis would ever agree to a peace deal which would result in them becoming, within a generation or two, a minority dependent on the goodwill of a Palestinian majority in a region without democracy or any real human rights.

In an interview with *Ha'aretz* in August 2000, Edward Said

was asked what would happen to the Jews if they became a minority in a single state: 'It worries me a great deal,' he said. 'The question of what is going to be the fate of the Jews is very difficult for me. I really don't know. It worries me.'

David Grossman told me, 'There is not enough reassurance in the galaxy for Israelis.' And there wasn't any reassurance, just a shrug of indifference.

And so we may have to face the nightmare that the war between the two peoples cannot be concluded; there is no deal that can ever be signed that will not give way, almost at once, to the resumption of the struggle. No US administration, however even-handed, can resolve or even impose a deal over land that can neither be shared nor divided. As long as the Israelis want a Jewish country, and as long as the Palestinians want the right of return, there can be no agreement. And there is no sign whatsoever of any movement of any significance in Israel against the idea of a Jewish country.

The flight home was a really bad journey, across the Mediterranean and the European continent. Across the other side of the aisle a ten-month-old Israeli baby, Netta, sat in her mother's arms smiling and gurgling, oblivious to the heavy storm winds we were passing through as we attempted to land in London, buffeted and blasted by gales and turbulence. I looked at her and, imagining her future, wondered if it would turn out that there were no solutions, only consequences, all of them tragedies.

Only yesterday, Yan emailed me with an afterthought. Did I know this old Israeli joke, which was, he thought, the true meaning of *davka*?

An American, a Frenchman and an Israeli get caught by an African tribe (as it usually is with stories of this kind). The chief tells them that they are going to be skinned and eaten and their skins will serve in building a canoe. Of course, they are given the right of the last wish. The American wishes for a bottle of whiskey, drinks it, gets skinned and eaten. The Frenchman wishes for a girl, receives her, does his deed, etc. The Israeli asks for a fork. The surprised tribesmen have no choice, and give him a fork. The Israeli repeatedly sticks in that fork all over his body, shouting, 'From my skin *davka* you won't make a canoe, bastards.'

It strikes me, writing this, that it might just as easily be a joke told by and about a Palestinian.

When I got home there was an invitation.

I was invited to chair the launch of a book, a little book, quite short, composed of the stories of Israeli writer Etgar Keret and a novella by Palestinian writer Samir el Youssef. They were roughly the same age. They grew up on each side of a border, Etgar as the son of Holocaust survivors who made their way from Europe to Israel in 1948, Samir as the son of refugees who fled their home to Lebanon the same year, and remain there today in a refugee camp near Sidon.

They had met at a conference of Israeli and Arab writers in Zurich. Etgar had quickly concluded that there were two groups of people there, himself and Samir, and everybody else.

They didn't talk to each other about politics. When I first met them, in the lobby of a hotel in central London a few hours before the launch of their book, *Gaza Blues*, Samir said, casually, 'By the way, Etgar, did you know that I'm in favour of a one-state solution?'

'Well, for me, it's okay,' Etgar replied. 'But listen, Samir, if the Israelis have to choose between a one-state solution and nuclear war, they'll choose nuclear war.' *Davka.*

There is a long tradition in literature of the anti-hero, the nebbishy klutz who wanders across the great battlefields of world history, dropping his gun, running away, questioning orders out of naivety or foolishness or false courage. The little man of literature is one of its most enduring qualities. For every Prince Hal, making speeches about St Crispin's day, there are thousands of Pistols, Bardolphs and Nyms. Keret's Israelis encamped in Lebanon were having stupid adolescent arguments with each other; they imagined that the Hezbollah had a new super weapon of giant rabbits with antennae on their heads; they worked in factories and rolled marbles into pipes that vanished, then crawled up the pipe themselves and found themselves in heaven, a boring heaven, where they got tired of the marbles that had arrived earlier.

In Samir's fictional refugee camp, Baseem wanders around trying to score some dope. He tries to get a visa to leave Lebanon and go to Germany, knowing that the travel agent is a crook and a liar, 'but I like listening to liars,' he says. The militants in the camp are revolutionaries full of hot air and piss. Baseem thinks he might marry his girlfriend and have twelve children, and then they can grow up to be martyrs against the Zionist enemy and the Zionist enemy will kill him, 'and we can get out of this fucking life.'

It turned out that Samir lived in the same neighbourhood as me in London, we were just walking distance away from each other. He had been in London for fifteen years, quietly writing, and when Etgar went home to Tel Aviv, Samir and I began to meet every couple of weeks for coffee, to talk: about writing, about literature, about the idiot politicians of Israel and Palestine, and the idiot activists who liked nothing better than to snatch away from us our complicated feelings about ourselves and hack them down into slogans.

One day he emailed me to say he had had an invitation to go to Israel.

Palestine! He had never set foot on its soil, not Jerusalem or Ramallah or Khan Younis. He was Lebanon born, and his mother came there when she was five years old, but still, almost all her life now, a refugee, with a child's memory inside her of home.

The invitation was from the Jerusalem Book Fair which had come up with a really hare-brained scheme to invite all kinds of writers from the region to meet together on a bridge at the crossing point between Israel and Jordan.

Mighty was the indignation of some of the rejection letters the organisers received! Normalise with the Zionist enemy? No chance. One writer said she needed an accredited record from each Israeli writer present that he or she had personally attempted to prevent the army from demolishing a Palestinian house before she would sit together on a platform in their noxious presence.

Still, Samir wanted to go, and I hoped very much he would accept, and he said he would go if I went with him, so I did.

A taxi driver was waiting for us at the airport. I could tell by his accent that he was originally from Poland. 'How did your family survive the war?' I asked him, automatically.

'That's a big story I have on my back,' he said.

We drove east to Jerusalem. He was like an Israeli from the early 1950s, still in love with Israel and with Zionism: 'Look at the beautiful tank!'

At the top of the hill, at the huge intersection, we were blocked by police cordons. Settlers were burning tyres on the road in protest against the disengagement. They were attacking the police and the police were dragging them off the asphalt into police vans.

'My god,' said Samir.

The next day we all piled into coaches and went off to the King Farouk Bridge, over the Jordan river. Our coach was full of publishers and literary agents and writers. More coaches were coming, from Tel Aviv and Haifa and other parts of Jerusalem.

We passed into Palestine. The landscape, familiar to me now, grew drier. Samir sat next to me silently, looking out of the window. I stayed silent too, except occasionally to point out the differing architecture of the West Bank, the flat-roofed Palestinian houses, the red roofs of the Jewish settlements.

After a while, I said, what do you feel about this? I expected him to tell me something about return, about home, about land, but he said, 'Nothing. It's interesting, but my grandparents were never here. They never even came to Jerusalem.'

The meeting at the bridge was the *balagan* you would have expected. Some came, some didn't. I was interested in an exchange between the Jewish-Israeli novelist A.B. Yehoshua and the Palestinian-Israeli Sayed Kashua, whose novel, *Dancing Arabs*, about a Palestinian-Israeli aping the Jews, trying to cut out the whole of his self that was Arab, made me very uncomfortable. Because what he had written, satirically, was a novel about what used to be called a self-hating Jew. It is a predicament of all minorities who want to take their place among the majority; do they take on its characteristics, assimilate to its culture and values, become the majority in their heads? And at what self-destructive price?

A.B. Yehoshua told the audience that a writer must write in his own language, not the language of the colonialist.

Sayed said, yeah, well. If you actually taught Arabic in the schools here then there would be a large enough market for literary fiction written in Arabic, but you don't teach it, you teach French.

But then another Palestinian-Israeli writer, Basilius Bawardi, said, hold on, Sayed, the reason you write in Hebrew is that it's the language of literary Modernism, which is suitable for writing about modern urban life, whereas Arabic is still a formal language. But some of us are trying to develop a Modernist Arabic, and why aren't you joining us?

In the afternoon, there was a discussion about whether artists could change the world, and everyone on the panel said they thought not.

But I believed that exchange in the morning was more to the point. If you put an Israeli and an Egyptian violinist together, you would find out that what they had most in common was the sheer torture of getting the strings of their instruments to do their bidding. 'How do you interpret the Tchaikovsky . . .?' And so on.

The war of words is one thing in the mouths of sloganeers; the writer's war with words is how to get them to make concrete that fine, shimmering thing that is in our heads and which falls away to nothing as soon as our fingers touch the printed letters on a keyboard.

The Palestinian writer Ahmed Harb told a story I liked a lot about how, when he was sixteen, during the Six Day War, the imam at the mosque in the village where he grew up, near Nablus, preached several times a day how the Israeli planes were falling from the sky like flies. The Jordanians had retreated to their rear position. On the horizon they saw tanks and jeeps approaching and cheered. The Jordanians had returned, to rescue them. But it was not the Jordanians. The Israeli commander raised his megaphone and issued an order: everyone was to return to their homes for curfew. Harb began to run, and kept running until he reached a cave on the outskirts of the village, a cave where, it happened, he had been born. He stayed there for three months. 'And I never returned to the mosque,' he said.

All writers prefer that cave to official propaganda.

Etgar, Samir and I did some readings, were interviewed for the radio, went to some receptions. Samir and I walked round the Old City. We stood above the holy site. I looked at the Wailing

Wall, he looked at the Al-Aqsa mosque. Feel anything, we asked each other? Nothing. We made calls on our cellphones to friends in London. Guess where we are? He bought a few souvenirs as gifts for friends, then we went and ate humus.

We met a taxi driver from Baghdad, speaking in Arabic on his radio to his brother, and Samir and he chatted for a few moments in that language. We arranged for him to take us to Tel Aviv.

Four days and four nights in Jerusalem were causing me to have breathing difficulties. I thought my head was going to explode, but Samir liked it. He thought he could live there, a city that had the drag of history behind it, where many tribes and faiths had passed through and left their mark.

We set off down the hill in the Baghdad driver's taxi and the sun came out and the trees of the Jerusalem hills were green. With the window open, I could begin to smell the sea, and the city.

We reached the road bridge across the Ayalon Highway, the demarcation point, for me, between Israel and that city home of mine, that supposing city, Tel Aviv. It is marked by the Azrieli Centre: two buildings, one a cylinder, one a triangle, white and many-windowed. There is supposed to be a third, a rectangle, but it's still a stump in the ground because Mr Azrieli has been locked, for years, in a battle with the city over zoning. Seen from the air, coming into the land, the three buildings are supposed to represent a child's wooden puzzle.

And there we were, the White City, dun-coloured now. Chaotic, dirty, home.

Ha ir, the city.

'Beirut!' Samir cried.

'What?'

'It's just like Beirut – excuse me, I don't mean it looks like it's in ruins . . .' But I knew what he meant: a Levantine city on the Mediterranean. Those places that have their back always turned against the land, like the port city I grew up in.

Samir was whisked around Tel Aviv by an old friend of his. She showed him Jaffa, Shenkin Street, the Bauhaus buildings of Rothschild Avenue, everything. Meanwhile, I met Michal and Thomas for coffee; we were joined by some friends of theirs out jogging. He was a member of the Israel Philharmonic. They talked about their son who was a member of the Divan Orchestra, put together by Edward Said, in the last couple of years of his life, and the Israeli Daniel Barenboim, composed of Arab and Israeli players.

The wife wanted me to meet a friend of hers, a Palestinian Christian woman in Bethlehem. She had had such an awful time since the start of the intifada, she said; their business had collapsed with the economy, and her husband was having an affair with an Israeli peace activist.

When I thought of who it should be that would take Samir on a guided tour of Israel, there was only one possible candidate, Ophir. He had come to one of our readings in Jerusalem. Samir had read from his novella, 'The Day the Beast Got Thirsty', and Ophir had sat in the audience, cracking up with laughter while everyone around him sat with their hands on their laps and solemn expressions on their faces, listening intently.

'Why were none of those fuckers laughing? It was fucking hilarious.'

'Oh, they think that because I am a Palestinian my whole life is nothing but suffering and anything I write is about suffering,' Samir said. 'We Palestinians are not allowed to have a sense of humour.'

I've never been sure about Arabic humour. Jewish humour, let's not display false modesty here, is the best in the world, but I never heard any Arabic jokes. We have, in Yiddish, a whole tradition of jokes about a numbskull and the numbskull always comes from a Polish town called Chelm. The fools of Chelm populate the stories of Isaac Bashevis Singer, and apparently there is a real place called Chelm which once had a Jewish population, though I never met anyone who said, 'Well, my grandparents came to America from Chelm,' because it's an association that makes people burst out laughing.

But according to Samir, Arabs also have their Chelm jokes, which makes me suspect that they are there in every culture, and there's a great book to be written by someone with a big budget, who would simply have to fly to the capital of any given country, walk into a café and ask, 'Do you know any jokes about a place full of stupid people?'

Now, according to Judah, the Palestinian Chelm is Hebron, which in Arabic is Hallil. But Samir said that in Lebanon the joke was about the people of a town in Syria, called Humus.

So he tells me this joke about two guys from Humus who are at the airport in Beirut. One of them says to the other, 'Look at the size of these planes on the tarmac. They're enormous! How could anyone hijack one of these, you couldn't get one under your arm.' His friend looks at him pityingly. 'You fool, you don't hijack them on the tarmac. You wait until they're up in the sky and then they're very small.'

Samir said he wanted to go north, to see Haifa and maybe Akko, the Crusader port. I asked him if he wanted to find his parents' village, but he said no, not this time.

Ophir and Ilana picked us up in Tel Aviv and we took off up the north–south highway. Ophir told Samir a lot of stories about the idiocy of the deputy mayor of Rannana and his plan to import bears from Africa, and Samir told Ophir a story of a Palestinian film made in the 1970s, which the whole family had watched in the camp, about some Palestinians who went into the Zionist entity armed with just a couple of Kalashnikovs and mowed down thousands of Israelis, 'except everyone knew that a Kalashnikov only has thirty bullets in the magazine, and

once you fired your thirty bullets you're finished, and these
Kalashnikovs were firing millions of bullets'. We were all laughing as we rolled north, on a sunny February day, and Samir
explained how in Lebanon everyone wanted a genuine Russian
Kalashnikov but most of the plebs just got Bulgarian ones. So
Ophir started with the story of him going to find his brother in
the army in Lebanon because no one had heard from him for a
while and everyone was worried sick, and when he eventually
tracked him down, there he was in a tent, rolling a huge spliff.

We drove through Haifa and went straight up the coast, to
Rosh Hanikra, the border with Lebanon. A sign on the wall had
arrows pointing in two directions: Jerusalem, Beirut. Ophir took
a photograph of Samir standing beneath it. Haifa was closer than
Beirut, he pointed out.

A bored Israeli soldier with a goatee beard and too-long hair
was sitting on a kitchen chair behind the barriers and fences
and barbed wire that separated the two countries. He was reading a John Grisham novel.

Ophir went over to him. 'You're a mess, look at you, I was never
allowed to have long hair and a beard when I was in the army.'

The boy looked back at him, 'Things have changed since you
old-timers were in the army, and, anyway, no one ever comes up
here except a UN vehicle a couple of times a month, so who
cares?'

Samir and Ilana had gone off somewhere; they had bought
tickets for the cable car which gave a spectacular view of the
coast. Ophir and I don't like heights, so we stayed behind in the
hot sunshine, sitting on a wall, talking. It was Saturday, and
secular Israel was out for the day. Many people were speaking
Russian. They were eating ice creams.

Samir and Ilana returned. She, the paediatrician, had divined
what was in his mind better than me, and she said, 'Let's just go
look for your parents' village.'

Lashuv. To return.

My grandparents fled from Poland and Russia and never looked back over their shoulders. My grandfather spoke of Warsaw, 'Varshaw' it was in his mouth. What a city, you never saw such a city! But he left Poland at the age of thirty, with his three children, and no one put a foot on Polish soil again.

I did. I went to the town where my father was born, Lomza, though I don't know if it actually was the town, or whether what he named as his birthplace was a regional authority. I found a quiet place in the middle of an agrarian plain through which a river ran. The earth was dusty with the bones of my ancestors, all along the river Bug. There was little left now to show that once there had been Jews there. The large synagogue in the town square had been dynamited by the Nazis in 1943; in its place was a small supermarket. A Jewish graveyard, stones, anti-Semitic graffiti, what had once been a Jewish neighbourhood, then a ghetto, a holding area for Jews waiting to be transported to Treblinka, a few kilometres away.

I came, I saw, I left. Our history, as Jews, had been that of continuous reinvention, something preserved in various forms, something tangibly Jewish in religion, cooking, rituals, traces going back through time of habits taken from a dozen different lands, always in transformation, always preserving the map of that long journey. Look at me, look at the face that stares back from the mirror with her pale freckled skin, dark hair, hazel eyes. Something genetic brought from where?

What is a Jew? What a question! Too complicated for all the isms and ologies and ites that roam around the world, seeking subservience to their doctrines. There is nothing neat or rational about us. Like a jigsaw puzzle piece, there is nowhere where we fully, seamlessly, fit in.

Tawoud. To return.

It was very close, the village, we only drove for about five minutes. Its name had been Bassa and now it is Betzel, a small quiet *moshav* with those distinctive red-roofed Israeli houses. There was a sign, in Hebrew, explaining its history. Ilana translated it. Yes, she said, the *moshav*, founded by Romanian refugees, had been built on the ruins of an Arab village.

Samir looked up at the hills that separated Israel from Lebanon. He knew these hills very well, but he had only ever seen them from the other side. Everything he saw, the landscape, the coast, he knew and recognised. This was home, not the dry landscape of the West Bank. After the Israelis came in 1948, his grandparents had fled their houses, only for a few days, they thought, and had walked over those hills to safety. For three weeks his grandmother had kept on returning to pick up pots, pans, sheets. Then one day she came back to find that the house had been cleaned out by the Bedouin.

He walked off a little way and, with his rented Israeli cellphone, called his mother, seventy kilometres away, in the refugee camp near Sidon, and told her where he was. We stood under the sign, trying not to eavesdrop.

No one was about. We drove along the *moshav*'s road for a few minutes and Samir said, 'My grandmother told me that there used to be an airfield.' We asked a boy on a bicycle if he could tell us where the airfield was, but he didn't know what we were talking about. We drove on and found its ruins. It was the remains of a British airbase from the Second World War. Stone arches in the ground were what was left of the underground hangars.

We left, and drove to Akko and had lunch, then went for coffee and sweet cakes where Arab men sat sharing hookahs. Ilana told Samir of her work in the hospital, of the Palestinian-Israeli children she treated, and the kids from Gaza she tried to fix up.

As for me, the whole country was reconfiguring itself inside my head. The map shook and shifted. The borders melted and changed. Samir's Palestine was not the West Bank and Gaza, his family had never been there. It was here, the north, the precise configuration of the landscape, those hills, that sea. It was not a political idea but a private attachment, as my own attachment to that city, Tel Aviv.

Lashuv (Hebrew), to return. *Tawoud* (Arabic), to return.

Samir had told me a little story as we walked through the streets of Jerusalem, about how, in his twenties, he had read a novel by Aharon Appelfeld, back in the days when the Palestinian national movement was reading Israeli writing as police readers, to track down the places where the Zionist enemy incriminated itself, and to take those precious quotes as weapons in its struggle.

The novel was about two boys running through Nazi Europe, escaping for their lives, and at the end of the novel they escape, they board a boat for Palestine. 'And I was relieved. And then I thought, how can you be relieved? They're coming to steal your country!'

This little anecdote, about literature, about its subversive power of empathy, about how listening to the story of the other has its own power, is what remains.

The Zionists made something, they made a country and a story. Everything exists for better or worse, but everything exists, the Israeli poet Yehuda Amichai wrote. It exists, that Israel, it cannot be undone.

The village of Bassa no longer exists, it can no more be resurrected than the Jewish life of Lomza. Still, the story of both these places continues, stubbornly persisting, winding through the decades.

We drove back to Tel Aviv. Everything looked different. The night air blew in from the sea. The people walking through the streets, along Ben Yehuda, past the Supersol, the synagogue,

Café Mapu, the silversmiths, the falafel café, the convenience stores – all looked more real than they had ever done before, more complicated, more interesting, more human. More frail and more tough, more of everything they were already, and even less capable of being the receptacles for slogans.

I saw my parents there, walking arm in arm, along the beach-front lights. I saw Samir's grandparents alighting from the bus that brought them south from Bassa. I saw Jaffa, I saw Jonah washed up on its shore from the whale's belly. I saw us all.

I knew I was among people who are not so pleasant and whom suffering has not improved. To love them is no easy thing, and so I thought that this is where I belonged, as a person who has come to understand that love is not a sentimental matter. Love is pain and loss. It must end in grief and mourning because we will close our eyes one day and our beloved will vanish for all eternity.

But only in this city does life for me exist in each of its three dimensions, our human tragedy with all its comic elements. And still it does.

Acknowledgements

First and foremost, I would like to thank Judah Passow, who, from the moment we first met in March 1998, has had an enormous influence on how I have thought and felt about this region, the two countries, Israel and Palestine, their people and their fate. It would never have entered my head to write this book without that chance meeting in Tel Aviv, and the many conversations we have had over the years. I would like to thank him for taking my innumerable early morning phone calls: checking dates, verifying the Hebrew word for this and that, making jokes and generally chewing over the news that came from his home country. This book is for him, and I hope that its readers will find their way to his marvellous photography, not just of this conflict but many others.

This book was also born out of two long conversations, first with Aharon Appelfeld and then with David Grossman, in Jerusalem in April 2003. I would like to thank both of them for sharing their time with me, and opening up their minds, and indeed their hearts. I am indebted to them for their friendship.

Next up, I want to thank Ophir and Ilana Wright, and Yan and Rosita, for their hospitality while I was in Israel, their friendship, their emails, the various attempts to educate a computer-illiterate, the rescue of the hard drive of my laptop after the Blaster Worm virus *balagan*, Yan for sending me the photograph that is on the cover of this book, and, above all, their great generosity in allowing their own lives to be shared with strangers. They are the best kind of friends you could wish for – the type who pick you up from the airport, deliver you back there and make suspicious phone calls on your behalf to find out if someone is really on the level.

Michal Yudelman and Thomas O'Dwyer ensured that no spare hour was wasted that could otherwise be spent drinking coffee and eating cake and yakking about politics and where to buy great jewellery and decoding the true dark intentions of Israeli politicians. May we go on arguing and shopping till eternity.

Ruth Ur, at the British Council, and her partner Phil Misselwitz, made parties, introduced me to Ruth's family, and tracked down the photographer who took the picture Yan had first found. Tel Aviv lit up for me with their presence.

I am most deeply indebted to Samir el Youssef, for allowing me to write about what is, after all, his own story of his return. Our conversations continue, week after week, here in London. I eagerly await his account. His voice, satirical, sceptical, yet above all humane and curious about others, resonates, I hope, in this book.

I'd also like to thank all who entered the Davka Contest: Daphna Baram, Risa Domb, Etgar Keret, David Passow, Hillel

Shenker, Eric Silver. Thank you for allowing me to reproduce your entries.

A version of the chapter 'Chutzpah' first appeared in the *Jewish Quarterly* and the *Guardian*. The chapter 'Pigua' first appeared in the *Guardian* unaltered. Versions of the chapters 'Sarut bamoach', 'Gush Katif' and 'Bu'ah' first appeared in the *Guardian*. I would like to thank Matthew Reisz, Ian Katz and Kath Viner for commissioning me.

Finally, my thanks to my agent Derek Johns, who rescued me with lightning speed from a tricky situation, and to my publisher, Lennie Goodings, whose editorial advice is, as ever, the best in the business.